▼

SPIKE LEE

w i t h

LISA JONES

PHOTOGRAPHY BY

DAVID LEE

A

FIRESIDE

BOOK

PUBLISHED BY SIMON & SCHUSTER INC.

NEW YORK LONDON TORONTO

SYDNEY TOKYO SINGAPORE

▼

mo'
B E T T E R
B L U E S

A SPIKE LEE JOINT

▼

Fireside

Simon & Schuster Building

Rockefeller Center

1230 Avenue of the Americas

New York, New York 10020

FIRESIDE and colophon are registered trademarks
of Simon & Schuster Inc.

Designed by Bonni Leon

Manufactured in the United States of America

10   9   8   7   6   5   4   3   2

Library of Congress Cataloging in Publication Data
Lee, Spike.
   Mo' better blues/Spike Lee with Lisa Jones; photography by David Lee.
     p. cm.
   "A Fireside book."
   Includes bibliographical references.
   1. Mo' better blues (Moton picture)   I. Jones, Lisa.   II. Title.
PN1997.M6353L44   1990
791.43'72—dc20   90-38532
                                        CIP

ISBN 0-671-72570-X

THANK YOU-THANK YOU-THANK YOU

As the locomotive picks up steam,
rolling over anything and everything
in our path, I would like to thank
folks for keeping us on the track.

Malaika Adero, Roger Armstrong, Barry Alexander Brown, Jheryl Busby, Ruthe Carter, CBS Records, Alice Coltrane and the Coltrane estate, Chuck D., Ossie Davis, Sean Daniels, Ruby Dee, Ernest Dickerson, Susan Fowler, Dennis Greene, W. C. Handy and the Handy estate, Preston Holmes, Jim Jacks, Pamm Jackson, Lisa Jones, Loretha Jones, Raymond Jones, William Kaplan, John Kilik, Sam Kitt, Arthur Klein, Sy Kornblitt, Alberta G. Lee, Bill Lee, the entire Lee family, Branford Marsalis, Tom Martin, Toni Morrison, Motown Records, Amy Olatunji, David Picker, Tom Pollock, Public Enemy, Robi Reed, Monty Ross, David Sameth, Zimmie Shelton, Carey Silver, Cynthia Simmons, Earl Smith, Wynn Thomas, Pat Tobin, Universal Pictures, and Tracey Willard.

CONTENTS

▼

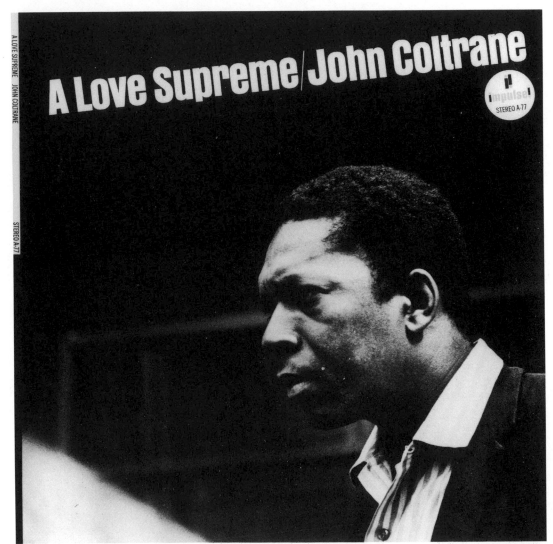

The album cover of *A Love Supreme* courtesy of MCA/Impulse!

No matter what . . . it

is with God. He is gracious and merciful.

His way is through love,

in which we all are. It is

truly—A LOVE SUPREME.

—John Coltrane

A Love Supreme used
through the courtesy
of the Coltrane family.

Robin Harris as Butterbean Jones.

▼

ROBIN HARRIS
1954 – 1990

My casting director, Robi Reed, woke me with a phone call early Sunday morning, March 18. Robin Harris had died in his sleep the night before. I got off the phone quickly to reflect.

We had held our second research screening of *Mo' Better Blues* in Philadelphia the night Robin passed. The audience loved Robin as Butterbean Jones, the country comic from wayback Mississippi. In fact, between the first research screening in Chicago, the week before, and the second, we restored some scenes with Robin that had been cut out for space reasons alone. We had to put them back in. Every time Robin appeared on screen, the audiences perked up, just waiting for him to open his mouth so they could roar. Robin Harris was a funny motherfucker.

Robin first came to my attention through Robi back in 1987. She kept telling me that I had to see this comic who was playing the Comedy Act Theater in L.A. Finally I saw him, and I was on the floor the entire night, having fallen out of my chair laughing. After that, every time I was in L.A. I caught Robin's act. He was a unique and brilliant talent. The thing I loved most about his comedy was it was *too Black*. I wrote the role of Sweet Dick Willie in *Do the Right Thing* for him. Let me backtrack: I cast him as Sweet Dick Willie—all the comedy was his own. I merely set up the situation, rolled the camera, and let Sweet Dick Willie be.

The spring of 1990 would have been a busy one for Robin. He was to tape a sitcom for CBS, embark on a national comedy tour, and release his first comedy album. We caught glimpses of Robin in Eddie Murphy's *Harlem Nights*, in Keenan Wayans' *I'm Gonna Git You Sucka*, and in an HBO comedy special. He had a major role in Reggie Hudlin's *House Party*, which was released just a couple of weeks before he passed.

Robin was thirty-six years young when he left us and it's certainly our loss. He was on the brink, the verge, of being *large*. One of Robin's favorite lines was "Ya gotta go, ya gotta go." I wish he didn't.

Spike Lee
March 19, 1990

▼

"Ain't that a bitch?"

▼

mo'
B E T T E R
FOREWORD

the year was 1929. The movie was the musical short *St. Louis Blues*. And the star was Bessie Smith. Bessie played a tough, no-nonsense, quick-tempered hot mama who clashes with a janitor, fights with a high-yellar strumpet out to steal her man, and then finds herself betrayed by that very dude, a slickster named Jimmy. The plot mechanics, of course, were shoddy, shamelessly stereotyped, and, well, let's admit it, rather trashily enjoyable. But when Bessie Smith opened her voice in song and let her big sound fill the screen, she turned the movie upside down, hoisted it onto her shoulders, and made *St. Louis Blues* a memorable experience. That same year Duke Ellington, dapper, smooth, and *clean*, appeared in another musical short, *Black and Tan* (directed by Dudley Murphy, who also directed Bessie's film). And Ethel Waters, once known to Black audiences as the slinky and slender Sweet Mama Stringbean, performed a jazzy pop rendition of her hit "Am I Blue?" in *On with the Show*. Today Bessie, Duke, and Ethel look as if they were ready to take American motion pictures off on something of a hip, rousing, soulful, giddy joyride. What they had done was to bring jazz—and also the idea of a jazz hero/heroine—to the movies. And they did so practically at the start of the sound era.

Sound movies had come into vogue only two years earlier, in 1927—when Al Jolson, his face smeared with burnt cork, had sung "Mammy" in a movie inappropriately called *The Jazz Singer*. Afterward the Hollywood studios rushed to release all-talking, all-singing musicals, going so far as to produce two all-talking, all-singing, all-colored productions in 1929: *Hearts in Dixie* and King Vidor's *Hallelujah*. And so from the very beginning, once the movies found their voice, American motion pictures responded to the power and force, the fierce beauty and poetry of Black sound. Yet, ironically, the movies seldom knew what to do with the African American artists who created such original sounds, particularly Black American jazz stars.

Has there ever been a figure as misused in the movies as the African American jazz star? American films have rarely had any place for Black jazz artists, other than on the sidelines, and these artists have been used mainly to pump up many a dud of a picture with some much-needed style and energy. Rarely have films cared about dramatizing the story of the Black jazz artist. Rarely, too, have films attempted to create the cultural tradition and community from which the music came. On those few occasions when a movie has focused on a Black jazz performer as star or lead character, I think Black audiences often have been dismayed and shocked that such a movie had been made not to speak to them but to reach some large White audience instead. The history of jazz in the movies (entertainment films, not documentaries) has been a long, sorry tale that reads like one of cultural displacement or arrested development.

After Ellington, Smith, and Waters worked in films, a dazzling lineup of other jazz artists came to the screen during the 1930s and 1940s: Louis Armstrong, Billie Holiday, Lionel Hampton, Hazel Scott, Count Basie, Jimmie Lunceford, Maxine Sullivan. In such films as *Stage Door Canteen* (1943), *Doctor Rhythm* (1938), *Going Places* (1939), *Reveille with Beverly* (1943), *Broadway Rhythm* (1944), *Atlantic City* (1944), *Pillow to Post* (1945), and *Rhapsody in Blue* (1945), the artists were brought on as specialty or novelty acts. They might perform a number or two, then disappear.

On those few occasions when the great stars were cast in actual roles, an audience might cringe at what they see. Billie Holiday played a maid in *New Orleans*. And poor Satchmo found himself singing about a skeleton in the closet or crooning "Jeepers Creepers" to a horse. Naturally, when the artists performed their music, their style transcended the racism of the movies. Surely, for Black audiences of the past, it must have been a thrilling experience to see these great performers, but, of course, frustrating to see them kept on the periphery.

By the 1940s, the jazz artist, particularly in the era of swing, had emerged as a distinctive cultural hero. Men like Ellington and Basie impressed Black audiences not only as supreme talents but also as social symbols: intelligent, skilled sophisticates in control of their careers as they overcame odds and broke down barriers within the entertainment world. Yet Hollywood movies made it look as if such jazz stars were not worthy of a story or film developed around them.

In the early 1940s, however, Hollywood briefly seemed infatuated with the idea of presenting a hip young master of music as a movie hero. But before American movies felt safe in exploring the psyche of the innovative jazz artist and incorporating his mystique and moody glamour into the iconography of commercial cinema, such a hero first had to undergo a slight transformation. He went from being an authentic homegrown cultural (racial) outsider (whose music invigorates the cultural mainstream) to being a movie myth/hero who was, shall we say, more palatable and clearly acceptable to the mass White movie audience: He became the rebel White boy with talent to burn or energy that wouldn't wait.

In 1941, Paramount released *The Birth of the Blues*, starring Bing Crosby as a young New Orleans lad who is so caught up with the colored man's levee music that he takes up the music himself, forming his own Dixieland band. Things really jell for the group once they hook up with Brian Donlevy, as a cat from Memphis who's a wild man with a horn. (*Variety* called the Donlevy character "An ofay who can toot like a Satchmo.")

That same year Warner Bros. released *Blues in the Night*, which focused on the struggles of a swing band whose members included Jack Carson as a trumpeter, Priscilla Lane as a singer, and Richard Whorf as a restless, lovestruck pianist. "For every note of music sounded in this movie," wrote the reviewer for *The Daily Worker*, "there's about a mile of melodrama. *Blues in the Night* says as little about real jazz as did *Birth of the Blues* earlier this week. But like Paramount, Warners had the sense to dub in enough hot music to give the customers some happy entertainment." As if to validate themselves, the films briefly brought in the sounds of Ellington, Armstrong, Ruby Elzy, and Jimmie Lunceford. Otherwise they would have been hollow to the core.

During the postwar era, Hollywood turned to tales of real-life jazz artists, their dilemmas and struggles. And again, in those musical movie biographies, the acceptable jazz/swing hero was a White one. No movie bios of Ellington or Armstrong or Basie. Instead there appeared those big-budgeted productions *The Fabulous Dorseys* (1947), *The Glenn Miller Story* (1954), *The Benny Goodman Story* (1955), and later *The Gene Krupa Story* (1959).

Today what's so intriguing about these movies is that the rebel artist/hero seems so tame and clean-cut, his experiences so sanitized and downright bland. At heart, the films are uplifting fables/parables: sometimes a Horatio Alger melodrama in which a poor boy makes good; sometimes also a half-baked morality tale in which the hero must battle the temptations of a loose woman before he ends up with his good woman; other times a familial struggle in which the musician is at odds with a parent or (in the case of the Dorseys) a sibling.

In those films, jazz itself is often viewed as a means of liberation: from a stuffy, nonchallenging, restrictive life and set of emotions; from the unbearable pretensions and inhibitions of an uptight culture. Sure, the White rebel jazz hero might have a hassle or two here or there, but always our fresh-faced, wholesome hero triumphs with his sweet girl-next-door-type lady. (She's June Allyson in *The Glenn Miller Story*. She's Donna Reed in *The Benny Goodman Story*.) The White jazz artist looks like a mighty peppy, well-balanced, and dutiful good guy without a real care in the world. Such lucky fellows. For them, jazz is never a real downer. Never do the creative juices drain them dry. Never does their art leave lasting psychological scars or psychic damage. They are just the right type of men to develop this all-American art form. Jazz/swing itself becomes part of a cheery, bourgeois life style.

An exception to this healthy portrait was Michael Curtiz's *Young Man With a Horn* (1950), which was inspired by the life and torments of Bix Beiderbecke. Here Kirk Douglas plays a heel of a trumpet player; his teacher, though, is a black man named Art Hazzard, played by the magnificent Juano Hernandez.

Interestingly enough, once Hollywood did turn its sights to making a movie about a real Black jazz figure, it chose to depict him also as basically a good-guy hero, caught up in an oedipal clash with an overbearing father and also struggling to decide between the sexy, loose big-city woman and the decent, wholesome girl back home. The picture that attempted to take the Black jazz artist mainstream was the 1958 *St. Louis Blues*, a biography of W. C. Handy.

Playing Handy was a miscast Nat King Cole. Also on hand were a very young and engaging Ruby Dee (as the pert ingenue Handy loves), Ella Fitzgerald, Pearl Bailey, Cab Calloway, the young Billy Preston (who plays Handy as a boy), and the great Mahalia Jackson. That mighty fortress of an actor Juano Hernandez played Handy's minister father, who is determined that his son steer clear of the devil's music.

Once out from under his pop's tight grip and ever ready to sow some wild oats and harness his talents, too, young Handy flips for a New Orleans lass, played by Miss Sultry Herself, Eartha Kitt. Of course, once we see Eartha as a too-hot-to-trot songstress, we know poor Handy is headed down a path of what could be

Photo from *St. Louis Blues* used by courtesy of Bettmann Archive.

Big city temptress (Eartha Kitt) woos W. C. Handy (Nat King Cole) in *St. Louis Blues* (1958).

▼

blissful iniquity. And ah, what a way to go! But tormented and guilt-ridden, Handy suffers from psychosomatic blindness—until the moment of redemption. The film naturally has a happy ending. When Handy's music is played in concert at the very proper Aeolian Hall, all this acceptance by the cultural establishment looks as if it brings Pop Handy to his senses. His son has not done so badly after all. Here, too, jazz was turned respectable with all the proper bourgeois trappings.

St. Louis Blues is not a very good film. No doubt because the film was conceived by White filmmakers, it offers no insight into the rich and varied cultural experiences that W. C. Handy drew from to create his music. It's too caught up in B-movie melodramatics and old-time Hollywood formula to be realistic. Yet it remains rather likable. On the rare occasions when it is shown today, Black audiences relish the sight of the legendary stars and often accept the melodrama with amusement. What emerges in the film, simply because it has a predominantly Black cast, is a lopsided sense of a Black community. In light of some of the jazz films that followed, it is now a pleasure to see Black characters at the center of the action and interacting and relating to one another rather than standing around in the wings to make some White star look good.

In 1958, *St. Louis Blues* also touched on, without fully examining, a valid subject: the life and troubles of the Black jazz artist. Soon Hollywood films would take the subject of the jazz hero a few steps farther and attempt to explore his position as the intellectual community's new-style mythic icon. By the late 1940s and 1950s, the view of the African American jazz star had changed drastically, due in large part to the appearance of bebop sensations. Men like Charlie Parker, Thelonious Monk, and, later, Miles Davis used their improvisatory skills to turn jazz inside out; they also created a whole new cool style for themselves. Just as important in the world of images, their personal histories (and that, too, of Billie Holiday)— their public tensions and conflicts and their very public declines—also redefined the position of the African American jazz artist. At the same time, postwar America's emerging concerns with the issue of racism also contributed to making the Black jazz artist a new kind of hero. Now he/she emerged as a metaphor for social inequities and racial injustices—the victim of a mean, debilitating, and exploitative system.

Early glimmers of this new image turned up in the 1960 melodrama *All the Fine Young Cannibals.* Pearl Bailey was cast as Ruby Jones, a self-destructive, boozy Bessie Smith–type blues singer who fixates on a young White musician played by Robert Wagner. The movie cannot make up its mind, though, what to do with Bailey and Wagner. Are they to be lovers? Or just buddies? About all we know for sure is that, Lord, Ruby sure loves the way that White boy plays that horn. Pearlie Mae herself seems much too sensible for this dim melodrama. And the film, no doubt to avoid controversy and to prevent us from asking too many questions, kills her off.

The first real sign of the new-style jazz movie hero was no doubt Sidney Poitier as Eddie Cook in Martin Ritt's 1961 *Paris Blues.* In this film Poitier and Paul Newman played two expatriate musicians living and working in Paris, away from the hassles and torments of American life. For Newman, Paris is a place where he can write his great jazz concerto. For Poitier, Paris is a city where he can be accepted as a man, not bound in by restrictions and racism. Into the lives of the two men come two young American women on vacation in Paris: Joanne Woodward and Diahann Carroll. Both men are now forced to make crucial decisions about their lives. Each must decide whether or not he will give up his life in Europe to return to the States with a good, decent woman.

Slow and rambling and without much heat or drive, *Paris Blues* tried to be a smoky, offbeat romance with some of the look and feel of France's new-wave films, then being shot on the streets of Paris. Today (and no doubt even in 1961), the film disappoints because it does not know what to do with its Black musician. Although the script toys with the idea of Eddie as a political rebel, it fails to develop the character, cannot explain to us his drives, his anxieties, his dismay and anger with his native country, which he believes has rejected him. Finally, the movie chooses to shift its focus from the compelling story of Eddie to that of the romance between Newman and Woodward, obviously making a concession to the large White movie audience.

Expatriate jazz musician Sidney Poitier meets Diahann Carroll, an American woman on vacation, in *Paris Blues* (1961).

▼

In *Variety*'s review of *Paris Blues*, the reviewer wrote: "It figures, for example, to fare better domestically in urban than in rural areas and in the North than in the South. The reaction of the Negro audience will be a factor. While this is likely to be largely favorable, since the film significantly erases some of the traditional color barrier of Hollywood product, it also might arouse some passive criticism from more radical quarters, where it may be felt that a potentially bold interracial theme has been abortively handled and cautiously diluted for mass consumption."

Variety seemed to realize, long before the Black movie boom of the early 1970s, the power and interest of an emerging new Black audience, which clearly looked at movies differently from the White audience. The Black audience would have preferred that *Paris Blues* focus on Poitier's character; that it address his racial, personal, and professional tensions; that it create a Black cultural context for him in which he would be seen relating more with other Black musicians rather than bonding with a White buddy (with whom the White audience identified) and isolating himself (and ultimately the Diahann Carroll character) from any semblance of a Black life. In short, *Paris Blues* failed to tell its story from a Black perspective. At the time, though, Hollywood had no interest in a Black perspective or the effect such a perspective might have on a Black audience.

Still, *Paris Blues* marked a start. Five years later, Sammy Davis, Jr., starred in *A Man Called Adam* as a tortured musician, a victim of a nasty, overbearing booking agent, of an insensitive music world, and of his own self-pity, a man we hoped to see redeemed by the love of a good woman. Then in 1967, the little-known *Sweet Love, Bitter* (based on the novel *Night Song* by Black writer John A. Williams) starred Dick Gregory as a self-destructive saxophonist named Richie "Eagle" Stokes (loosely modeled, so it seemed, on Charlie Parker), who burns out on too much booze and dope. While both films were interesting projects, neither could create enough of a vital community that the Black audience could identify with. Surely, those few Black audiences that saw *Sweet Love, Bitter* must have felt a bit cheated, for it stressed the friendship of Gregory's character and a young White man. At the same time, these films, in tone and mood, rhythm and perspective, could not find stylistic cinematic equivalents for the musical style of jazz.

Oddly enough, the jazz biography that Black audiences responded to most was a movie that has been criticized (justifiably) as being untrue to the details of its subject's life and that miscast a striking performer in the lead role. That film was none other than *Lady Sings the Blues*, an engrossing, old-style, old-fashioned melodrama with skinny, extroverted, live-wire Diana Ross playing the moody, still, "quiet-fire" Billie Holiday.

Much of the success of *Lady Sings the Blues* with Black audiences (and White ones, too) can be credited to its entertaining view of a Black community. The real Billie Holiday operated in a world of Black and White: She helped integrate the nation's top clubs, and, of course, she appeared with Artie Shaw's orchestra. The movie does not really have a handle on this aspect of Billie's experience, the disorienting effect the White clubs and managers and, sometimes, audiences had on her.

But I think the Black audience responded to the unabashed romance of the film (finally a Black man and woman on screen can peer into one another's eyes and float off in a dream) and also to the vital interplay of leading lady Ross with her fellow Black actors. Perhaps because it sprang from Motown, the film captured some of the spirit and camaraderie of the music world. Billy Dee Williams really does look like one of those slick dudes who hung around the clubs and drove the ladies wild. As Piano Man, Richard Pryor is able to summon up a portrait of a man with his ethnic juices flowing, as he kids and soothes Lady Day in language and movement that strike a Black audience as real and true. Sometimes it seems as if Pryor is nudging Ross, as if to tell her, "Now, come on, let's be real, sister." She seems to get the message, too. While it is often hard to think of Diana Ross as anyone other than Diana Ross, she creates nonetheless a vivid screen heroine who turns tragic but who also knows how to enjoy herself. To her credit, Diana Ross never lets her Billie Holiday become a pathetic loser. And that is something the Black audience continues to love about the film, no matter how much the music establishment criticizes it.

Films such as *A Man Called Adam; Sweet Love, Bitter;* and *Lady Sings the Blues* were all trying hard to say something new. What they did was to significantly alter the movie image of the Black jazz artist. Now, at least, he/she was a person with identifiable problems and tensions, at odds with society and at war with himself or herself as well. Never again would the Black jazz artist be thought of as some happy-go-lucky peripheral figure. If anything, his/her troubles demanded that he/she be placed center stage.

Yet that tradition—of the Black jazz hero/heroine as troubled, brooding victim—has continued, most notably in two celebrated films of the 1980s, Bertrand Tavernier's *Round Midnight* and Clint Eastwood's *Bird*. Today, for some jazz aficionados, the two are *the* jazz films. Many would have us believe that the jazz film has finally come of age, as if the problem of perspective that plagued previous portraits of African American jazz artists had miraculously vanished.

Yet, interestingly enough, both films, while admittedly admirable in what they hope to do (provide us with some serious comment on the Black jazz artist's tension with a culture that appears to have no place or appreciation for him), have not reached the mass Black movie audience, and I think that may be because, lauded as the films are, they tell us next to nothing about their heroes as Black men. Neither film seems to understand or have any interest in where their heroes come from or the forces that have shaped the men, the unique African American culture that has stamped or defined them. Neither film has much vitality. And both films, rather than celebrating their heroes, are sad-eyed elegies that begin on one low note and end on another.

Directed by French filmmaker Bertrand Tavernier with a script by Tavernier and David Rayfiel, *Round Midnight* tells the story of saxophonist Dale Turner, a tragic hero from the very first frame. In 1959, Turner has left the States to live in Paris, where he finds work and artistic acceptance, so we are to believe. Turner, however, is a weary, alienated, troubled man, never at peace. Dominated and treated almost like a child by his woman, Buttercup, Dale stoically goes through the motions of living and sometimes, it seems, through the motions of performing. Around him are other Black musicians, but they are presented as such a low-key, somber, rather dreary bunch that is it any wonder poor Dale doesn't seem to spend much free time with them?

Obviously, the director wants us to feel no one understands Dale. That is, of course, until a Frenchman named Francis (played by François Cluzet) shows up. We first see him in the most romanticized of images: He is crouched outside the club where Dale performs, listening intently in the rain to the artist he considers a god. Once he meets Turner, the noble, sensitive Francis is determined to save this man. And we watch him as he rescues Turner from one crisis after another, at one point feverishly racing through the streets of Paris and combing the city's hospitals in search of the man when he has mysteriously disappeared. Francis is a very brave, plucky fellow. He is even willing to confront the formidable and testy Buttercup.

A commercial artist who is separated from his wife and lives with his young daughter, Francis soon takes Dale into his home and dedicates himself to him. (He even borrows money from his estranged wife to get a larger apartment.) Just so we will not forget Francis's dedication, the camera seems to delight (in a bittersweet, melancholic way) in showing dear Francis giving old Dale tender, sensitive glances.

And so the film has us believe that Francis does have restorative powers. A healthier and more vital Dale seems to be getting back on his feet, so much so that he returns to the States for club appearances. Francis, naturally, accompanies him, meets with the manipulative manager of the club where Dale is booked to perform, stays at the hotel with Dale, meets Dale's lovely young daughter (who is named Chan; this is Tavernier's tribute to Charlie Parker's Chan), and suspiciously eyes the Black dope pusher who hangs around, waiting to move in on Dale.

But aware that America is all wrong for Dale, Francis finally tells his friend he is returning to Paris; he has a reservation for Dale to join him on the flight. But Dale never shows, and he ends up dead in the States, done in by the corruptive forces of a country and culture that never appreciated him in the first place.

Round Midnight has some moving moments and at times its melancholic tone casts a hypnotic and oddly affecting spell. What distinguishes the film most is the majestic presence of Dexter Gordon, who plays Dale Turner with great reserves of wit and ironic detachment. Dexter knows a whole lot more than he is saying.

But the movie is misconceived from the word go. And as much as some audiences may like the *idea* of the film, I think it becomes very difficult for Black audiences to fully connect to it, primarily because of its rather self-righteously lopsided point of view, which clearly springs from a White European consciousness. *Round Midnight* has no desire to establish some sense of a Black community —some comment on an African American cultural tradition—that a Black audience could identify with. The movie never tells us where Dale has come from. And it steadfastly refuses to establish relationships for Dale with other Black characters.

Round Midnight throws in a scene or two, in particular a party at Francis' apartment, where we can see Dale relaxing with other Black artists. But such sequences are the most unfelt, the most false, almost humorless and devoid of energy. The director has no idea how Blacks relate to one another, the type of humor and pull and tug that enlivens conversations, the connective cultural tissue (the set of references, the use of language, the body rhythms themselves) that would make these people feel so much at home with one another. At best, the party sequence is simply used as part of the elegy, as if a Dale Turner never had a highfalutin, really good time in his life. He just seems defeated throughout.

The Black character closest to Dale is the demanding Buttercup. Here the film does something terrible to Black women. As Buttercup, Sandra Reaves-Phillips is turned into Dale's dour and meanspirited nursemaid, his jailkeeper, his hefty mammy. Throughout most of the film, she argues, berates, or picks at him. Never can we imagine what brought the two together in the first place. Worse, we never have a moment when the two connect. (The film also unpleasantly contrasts the brown-skinned Buttercup with the character played by Lonette McKee, who is used mainly as some sort of high-yellar dream goddess, all sweetness and light and beautiful adornment during her very brief appearances.)

Curiously, there is a moment in the film when Sandra Reaves-Phillips breaks loose from the director's firm grip. In a party sequence, she exhibits an unexpected sexy kick and punch when she sings Bessie Smith's bawdy number "Put It Right Here." You almost start to like her. But the film depicts her as the bad wife so that the noble Francis can be the good mistress.

I think for those Black audiences that saw the film it became distressing that the director could not give us some insight into Buttercup, what she has endured from Dale or the love within her that makes her want to protect him (the type of love that is so passionately defined when it comes from a White woman in *Bird*).

Certainly, there have been classic cases of Black women married to jazz artists who felt they had to take charge of their husbands' business matters, had to shield and insulate them from the hangers-on and the constant, often agonizing craziness of the music world. Interestingly, in the documentary *Straight, No Chaser*, we see how Thelonious Monk's wife cared for him and managed his affairs, ever alert, it seems, to the sharks who infest the waters. Theirs appears to have been a real marriage in which the two partners understood and valued one another. (We also see a real jazz artist who, though troubled, sometimes has a wild, merry twinkle in his eyes and an offbeat way of looking at things that makes him a very disarming man.) But none of that happens in *Round Midnight*.

Round Midnight is dedicated to Bud Powell and Lester Young and is inspired by "incidents in the lives of Bud Powell and Francis Paudras." (Paudras was a Frenchman who befriended Powell—indeed, even took him into his home.) We all know that, from the days of Josephine Baker and Sidney Bechet to the present, Black artists have indeed found warm acceptance abroad. But Francis, as a metaphor for Paris and its affection for Black artists, is rather absurd. And the film itself often looks like a fundamentally self-righteous wish-fulfillment drama that is hell-bent on telling us that only a sensitive European sensibility could understand or respect a Black jazz artist. In some respects, the movie becomes a tale of interracial male bonding, similar to Hollywood films of the '80s, which led us to believe there were no racial differences or distinctions, that racism did not exist.

Bird suffers from similar problems. It, too, is an overextended elegy. It's one long rainy night of a movie that focuses so much on its hero's angst and pain that it cannot muster up enough energy or insight to let us see what Charlie Parker's art derived from. And ultimately it becomes so drawn out and humorless that its hero, despite Forest Whitaker's rather measured performance, becomes something of a dreary sad sack.

Bird, of course, records the story of Kansas City jazz saxophonist Charlie Parker, who, in the 1940s, along with Dizzy Gillespie, Thelonious Monk, and Bud Powell, was considered one of the fathers of bebop. To his fellow musicians and fans, Parker had the nickname Yardbird, later shortened to Bird. The story went that on an occasion when the car Parker was a passenger in accidentally hit a chicken, he insisted that the driver turn around and get the bird for their dinner. The story itself captures some of his wild-man spirit, his very crazy/practical point of view. But Parker had another side: He was a driven, restless, self-destructive genius of an artist who burned out on women, booze, and dope. In 1955, he was dead at the age of thirty-four.

Anyone with any desire to know more about Charlie Parker, however, will not find it in Clint Eastwood's somber movie. Rather than presenting us with a straightforward, chronologically ordered narrative (which, although not experimental, at least might make sense), *Bird* jumps all over the place and often looks like little more than a series of loosely connected, unformed flashbacks. The movie doesn't take time to ground us in the experiences that shaped Parker. Instead it hops a route similar to that of *Round Midnight*.

Whereas *Midnight* pays tribute to the tribulations of Turner's self-sacrificing White buddy Francis, *Bird* salutes the tribulations of the last woman in Charlie Parker's life, Chan Richardson. Vividly played by Diane Venora, Chan is a warm, generous woman, Parker's keeper, his friend, public defender, soul mate, and main link to life—just the right type of heroine for the vast White audience to identify with.

And it is here obviously that the movie, for Black audiences, goes disastrously wrong. Watching *Bird*, one would never know that there were other important Black women in his life. It was Parker's mother who gave him his first instrument at age eleven. As a teenager, Parker had an early marriage in Kansas City. In an interview in the documentary *Celebrating Bird: The Triumph of Charlie Parker* (directed by Gary Giddins and Kendrick Simmons), Parker's first wife, Rebecca, poignantly speaks of the young Parker's drug problem and of the day when he asked her to let him out of the marriage. According to Rebecca Parker, her young husband said to her, "Rebec, would you free me, please? I believe I could become a great musician if I were free." It is a simply stated and highly moving moment that says something about a relationship between a talented Black man and a Black woman that films like *Bird* and *Round Midnight* come nowhere close to

MO'
BETTER
BLUES

comprehending. And it is such a moment that I believe Black audiences yearn to see in films, particularly about artists like Parker.

Bird also cannot give us any feel for Parker's close relationship with Dizzy Gillespie or other Black musicians. Yes, we see Dizzy and Bird together, exchanging words and affection in tepid scenes that appear perfunctory at best. We never sense that these men have endured a set of shared experiences on the road or in performance that connects them, nor do we sense that, when together, their music saves, invigorates, distinguishes them. The movie doesn't build or expand on their relationship, doesn't explore its complexity and depth or the changes it undergoes.

Interestingly, the moments of true camaraderie (and some emotional intensity) are reserved for Parker and the White musician Red Rodney. It is Rodney whom Parker warns of the dangers of drugs, to whom he says, "If I ever hear about you using this shit, I will come from my grave and I will haunt you." It is Rodney whom Parker teams up with in some of his lighter moments: a Jewish wedding at which he plays; a tour through the segregated South where Parker passes Rodney off as a Black blues singer called Albino Red.

When Red Rodney meets Parker, he quickly informs the saxophonist of his hero worship. "I took the job touring with Krupa," he says, "instead of staying in Philadelphia because the tour came to L.A. and I knew you were going to be here." In this scene, *Bird* wants us to believe that the White Rodney appreciates the greatness of Parker (as does the White Chan) in a way that we do not see displayed by the Black characters. In fact, Parker's great humiliation comes when, as a kid, he plays before a Black audience that fails to appreciate him. (A cymbal is thrown at him. It's used as an image that haunts him all his life.) And throughout he is resented by the jealous Black musician Buster Franklin.

By spotlighting the positive aspects of his relationships with Chan and Rodney, by refusing to tell us anything significant about the very young Parker, by staying clear, too, of any serious examination of the racism within the music business and the jazz clubs, the film strips him of his roots and denies the very cultural experiences that defined him and his music, and the social/political system that may well have contributed to his self-destructiveness.

Its greatest failing, though, like that of *Round Midnight*, is that it cannot set up a Black cultural context for its central character. As a result, the audience that should connect most to such a film, the Black movie audience, finds itself frequently intrigued by the subject but alienated by its treatment. Because the heroes of these films are so culturally and emotionally muted, jazz itself seems robbed of its voice, its spirit, its point of view. I am not saying that a Black audience cannot enjoy parts of such films, but our level of identification can go but so far. These movies have worked us up emotionally but the emotion is directed against the films, rather than with them, for, deep inside, too many of us feel too much has been left unexplained, unexplored, unexamined.

In essence, these films fundamentally have been made for White audiences. I think on a certain level the films also make White males (who identify with a Francis or Rodney) feel good about themselves; their guilt feelings about racism are often assuaged.

And so now comes Spike Lee's *Mo' Better Blues*, which I think will be a real surprise for audiences, who will find the differences between this film and past jazz dramas striking. For here we have a jazz film from a fresh perspective: that of a young African American filmmaker, who responds to jazz's rhythms, moods, and textures—and who understands the place of the jazz hero within the consciousness of the Black community. He also understands that community itself. And no doubt what will be most exciting and invigorating for the Black audience (and let us hope for the White audience, too) is the way the film captures the Black community's vitality and diversity. Here we see a jazz hero who does not operate in some cultural vacuum. Nor does he bond with some White buddy. Nor does the film make concessions to grab the attention of the mass White audience. Instead there are cultural signposts and demarcations all over the place.

From the very start of *Mo' Better Blues*, we are introduced to the world from which the hero, Bleek Gilliam, comes: the family, the friends, the clubs, the sounds, the conflicting drives of a diverse set of personalities. Whether we see Bleek with Giant or with Shadow or with his spirited father, Big Stop, or with the two independent women in his life, Indigo and Clarke, the movie swiftly and ingeniously establishes a network of relationships—some simple, some complex —between Bleek and other Black characters. Throughout there is a fast-moving interplay of faces, voices, rhythms, styles, and a new kind of cultural authenticity. When the characters speak, they do so sometimes in a kind of shorthand that is a relief from the type of fake pseudohip jazzy dialogue the movies so long have favored. And they do not have to attitudinize or pose and posture to let us know they are Black. Instead they are blessed with a natural cool, an inbuilt assurance and awareness of who they are and the culture from which they come.

Yet one should not think that *Mo' Better Blues* presents an idealized world. As Spike Lee did so dexterously with *She's Gotta Have It*, he dramatizes for us not only the cultural links and similarities of his characters but also the rivalries, jealousies, and infighting, revealing to us the complex diversities within the African American community. And we have a sanely sexual hero who must balance the demands of his art, his profession, and his personal life. He also has to look at the Black women in his life in a new way.

I think *Mo' Better Blues* wants to take us in a whole new direction. It's almost as if its filmmaker had met up with Bessie, Duke, and that feisty old Ethel and said, "I know what you're about. I understand what you were trying to do." He wants to keep us on that soulful, moody, enlightening joyride that that dazzling, gifted trio started us out on more than sixty years ago.

Donald Bogle

INTRODUCTION

W E ' R E   A   W I N N E R

Nineteen hundred and ninety and the Mo' Better makes it Mo' Better. Being the son of a jazz musician and composer, it makes sense that I would make a jazz film. The question was when. I have to thank Clint Eastwood and his film *Bird* for making *Mo' Better Blues* the follow-up to *Do the Right Thing*. I try to set my own agenda and standards, so I never once thought about the pressure of topping *Do the Right Thing*'s critical and commercial success. What was important to me was not to repeat myself.

This time out, I chose to explore male/female relationships. All artists are driven by love for their art, and great artists are selfish in their devotion to it. This is Bleek Gilliam to a T. His music is his number one. So where do the women (two) in his life fit in? How do Clarke and Indigo deal with the fact that he is seeing both of them at the same time? And how does he tell them that they will always be second fiddle to his trumpet? That's some cold shit, and it takes a strong woman to stay with a man like that. Okay, okay, I know you're wondering if this Bleek character is Spike. All I can say is I love film more than Bleek loves his music.

Mo' Better Blues is our first film of the '90s. By we, I'm talking about Forty Acres and a Mule Filmworks. The crew: co-producer Monty Ross, cinematographer Ernest Dickerson, music composer Bill Lee, production designer Wynn Thomas, casting director Robi Reed, and costume designer Ruthe Carter. We've been working together since *School Daze*, some of us before that. Of course, these aren't all of the folks, but they're the nucleus. It's great to see us grow with each film. You can't do better than that. You gotta grow or you go.

Ten years ago, when we were students at Morehouse College, my right hand Monty and I would sit on my grandmother's porch during those hot Atlanta summers and visualize what we are doing now: making films about, and for, Black people, first and foremost. Our mission is not meant to exclude anyone else, it's just what we've been called to do.

We have provided employment for young Black talent, in front of and, more importantly, behind the camera, since *She's Gotta Have It* in 1986. I've been accused of hiring only Blacks, which is not the case. My goal is to give work to as many qualified Blacks as I can. If you've spent any time around film sets, you know that, for the most part, they're lily-white. One reason for this is that film unions are notoriously closed units. We have been able to get twenty-five Blacks into the unions because of *Do the Right Thing* and *Mo' Better Blues* alone, and we're not stopping there.

As Forty Acres and a Mule heads into the '90s, I think back to what has propelled us. For me, a driving force has been hating to lose. I've had a competitive spirit since I was very young. Though I wasn't the biggest, strongest, or fastest, I was always the leader of our block's softball, stickball, and football teams. Even back then, I hated to lose: stoopball, checkers, chess, Strat-O-Matic, whatever.

Up until high school, I actually thought I would be a major league baseball player. I must have been nuts, but I believed it. Even though I don't have the physical skills, I still think I have the heart. When the reality set in that I was not going to be a pro athlete, I got into film. I have transferred all my competitiveness to film, and I go about making films as if I were the underdog, the team no one believes will win.

One thing about sports, when a team gets a big lead, it must struggle to keep it up. When you have your foot on your opponent's neck, not only do you have to keep it there, but you've got to put your other foot there too. You have to go all out each time. And you can't measure your worth by the awards you didn't win, or the Academy Award nominations you didn't receive. You yourself know what you've accomplished and what you haven't.

For all great teams or dynasties, like the Yanks, 49ers, Lakers, UCLA, it's about longevity. The long run. It's not about being a flash in the pan, a spring-training phee-nom, or the appointed Negro for the moment. It's about what we've started: four films in the last five years:

She's Gotta Have It	1986	*Do the Right Thing*	1989
School Daze	1988	*Mo' Better Blues*	1990

It's our challenge to keep this shit up, because I hate to lose.

▼

D O   T H E   R I G H T   T H I N G

We wuz robbed at Cannes: From left, with Cinque Lee *(partially obscured)*, Richard Edson, Ossie Davis, Ruby Dee, and Joie Lee in front of the Grand Palais at Cannes.

▼

Do the Right Thing was the critical and popular choice for Best Film at the 1989 Cannes Film Festival. We were looking forward to the Grand Prize, or to something, at least. Two hours before the awards ceremony, we gathered in Universal executive Nadia Bronson's suite as she called Gilles Jacob, head of the festival, for the results.

I watched Nadia as she talked to Jacob on the phone. Her face grew long, and I knew we were in trouble. "Not anything? Not anything?" she said, then she hung up the phone. "Spike, you didn't win anything," she told me, "not a thing." I was crushed. While discussing whether or not we should attend the ceremonies, Ossie Davis and Ruby Dee walked in, smiling and dressed elegantly. When I told them the bad news, Ossie had to sit down. He was more hurt than I was.

Ten films won prizes, but we were overlooked, passed over altogether. Sally Field was the only juror who fought for the film. Even Hector Babenco, the director of *Pixote*, one of my favorite films, fronted on us. The German filmmaker Wim Wenders, president of the jury, was said not to have liked the fact that it's my character, Mookie, who throws the garbage can through the window of Sal's Famous Pizzeria. Apparently Wenders considered it an unheroic act. Somewhere deep in my closet, I have a Louisville Slugger baseball bat with Wenders' name on it.

▼

Do the Right Thing jumped from the movie section to "NBC Nightly News," "The Oprah Winfrey Show," "Nightline," and the editorial pages of newspapers across the country.

▼

▼

John Grimes. Reprinted by permission of John Grimes.

Jack Ohman. Reprinted by permission: Tribune Media Services.

o n e

THE mo'

BETTER

always knew I would do a movie about the music. When I say the music, I'm talking about jazz, the music I grew up with. Jazz isn't the only type of music that I listen to, but it's the music I feel closest to.

I saw *Bird*, Clint Eastwood's portrait of Charlie Parker, in the fall of '88. Bertrand Tavernier's *Round Midnight*, which was released two years before, was a slightly better film, if only because of saxophonist Dexter Gordon's performance. Both were narrow depictions of the lives of Black musicians, as seen through the eyes of White screenwriters and White directors. Two of the three main characters in *Bird* are White. And of all the accounts of Parker's life that Eastwood could have based the film on, he chose a book written by Bird's White wife, Chan Parker.

Every jazz musician I know hated *Bird*. There was not a moment of humor in the film. Max Roach, who played with Parker, told me that he was the funniest person he ever met. You would never have guessed it from watching *Bird*. Not only was the tone grim, but the film was so dark you couldn't see a damn thing. It seemed like it was raining half the movie. On all fronts, *Bird* just rang false.

Shortly after seeing *Bird*, I read that Woody Allen was planning a film about jazz. Now, wait a minute! First Clint Eastwood, and now Woody Allen! You know I couldn't let Woody Allen do a jazz film before I did. I was on a mission.

One look at *Bird* and *Round Midnight* told me what not to do, but I still had to figure out what kind of jazz film I wanted to make. Despite the problems I had with *Bird*, I realized that any film based on Charlie Parker's life would be open season for criticism. Audiences bring excess baggage to films based on the lives of real people. Folks were bound to walk out of the theater saying, "I knew Bird, he didn't hold his horn like that," or "He didn't wear his hat like that." I decided to stick with fictional characters in *Mo' Better Blues*, knowing that it would give me more freedom as a writer.

Period pieces about jazz have been done before. Though in this day and age the idea of a jazz film almost implies period piece, I always knew that *Mo' Better Blues* would take place in the present. I wanted to show that there are young jazz musicians out there today who are carrying on a tradition. At the same time, I didn't want to do a film that was about jazz exclusively, though I knew the script would center on characters who were jazz musicians.

I came up with the scenario of a jazz musician who is very honest with his two women friends. He tells each that she is not the only woman in his life, and that his music is more important to him than their relationship. I decided that this character would be a trumpet player, because the image of the jazz saxophonist had been used too often, and I named him Bleek, which is the nickname of my uncle Richard, a good friend of my father's since Morehouse.

Before I wrote one word of *Mo' Better Blues*, I knew I wanted Denzel Washington to play the lead. In the fall of '88, Denzel was starring, with Ruby Dee and Paul Winfield, in *Checkmates* on Broadway. I went to see the play a couple of times. The minute Denzel appeared on stage, the women in the audience started to scream. Not only was Denzel a great actor, but he was a legitimate matinee idol. I wanted to write a role for Denzel that Black women were waiting for him to play. He has done a number of important co-starring roles in films like *A Soldier's Story*, *Cry Freedom*, and *Glory* (which earned him an Oscar for best supporting actor). And he has played a leading man in *The Mighty Quinn* and *For Queen and for Country* (an independent film produced in England). But he still hadn't done a bona fide romantic lead. *Mo' Better Blues* would be his chance.

So, I had my foundation: It would be a jazz film, set in a contemporary context, with fictional characters and Denzel Washington as the leading man. I took notes from Christmas '88 until early April, then wrote the first draft.

While taking notes for the script, I read the jazz bassist/composer Charles Mingus' autobiography *Beneath the Underdog*. Though the book didn't influence the content of *Mo' Better Blues*, I did like the title, so that's what I named the jazz club. Around this time, Malaika Adero at Simon & Schuster passed me a copy of the advance galleys of *Miles: The Autobiography*, written with Quincy Troupe. The book helped put me in a jazz mode. Just the way Miles talked was funny as shit.

I did slip one of Miles' stories into the film. Miles once yelled at a musician for playing the wrong notes. If you want to play your own notes, he told him, go the fuck outside, play them, and come back when you're done. Bleek says something similar to his saxophone player, Shadow Henderson, who has his own ambitions to start a band.

Branford Marsalis, the saxophonist/composer, is a good friend of mine. Since Branford is part of the young generation of jazz musicians that inspired the film, I thought his views on the music and recent jazz films would be helpful in bringing Bleek to life. I did a long interview with Branford between the first and second drafts of the script. He graciously invited me out on the road with his band, but things started to pick up with the film, and I couldn't find the time.

I worked out early in my notes that something life-threatening would happen to Bleek at the end of the film. I've always read about athletes who get injured and can't play again. I wanted to apply this scenario to a musician's life. If your entire life is dedicated to your music, what happens when you can't play anymore? If playing music is all you ever wanted to do, what you believed you were put on this earth to do, how do you go on living? How do you start again?

Bleek wasn't in love with the trumpet when he was young, but what started out as a curse for him became an obsession. In the first draft of the script, Bleek gets hit in the face with a garbage can, which puts a cap on his trumpet-playing days. By the second draft, I decided someone would hit Bleek in the mouth with his own trumpet. I thought it would be mo' symbolic to have the thing that he loves most be the thing that ends his career.

Bleek's obsession with his music makes him a great musician, but it also makes him selfish. He won't play songs written by the guys in his band, he only plays his own music. He makes it clear to his women friends that they don't matter as much as his music. Tragedy forces Bleek to turn his life around. When people come close to dying, they call on God. "I know I've been wrong," they say, "I know I've been an asshole, but if you let me get out of this one, I promise to be a better person." That's what happens to Bleek. I've never been in that position myself, but when I was young I did have bad asthma. We all tend to take good health for granted. It takes being sick to make you realize how lucky it is just to be healthy.

Mo' Better Blues is not a love story. I find love stories corny, and I try not to make corny movies. This is a film about relationships—Bleek's relationships with his manager, his father, his band, his two women friends, and his music. *Love Supreme*, the original title of the film, came from jazz giant John Coltrane's famous album *A Love Supreme*, recorded in 1964. The album is one long composition arranged in four parts: "Acknowledgement," "Resolution," "Pursuance," and "Psalm." It's a very spiritual work and I used it as inspiration for the film. The love in *A Love Supreme* goes beyond romantic love. It's love for God and the human community.

I decided to use the first part of *A Love Supreme*, "Acknowledgement," at the end of the film in a montage that shows Bleek getting his life back together after the accident. Though John's widow, Alice Coltrane, did not grant me rights to the title, she did allow me to incorporate the song as I intended, which I'm thankful for.

One day I want to write a book collecting every single expression for making love. There must be a million of them. Number one on my list is *the mo' better*. Toward the end of production, it became evident that I wouldn't be able to use the title *Love Supreme*. I began to think. (Of course, everyone and his mother suggested alternatives.) What about *Variations on the Mo' Better Blues?* It sounds like the title of a jazz composition. After much prodding from Universal chief Tom Pollock, my father, and friends, I shortened it to *Mo' Better Blues*.

I got the term *mo' better* from a friend from D.C., Patti Hailes. Patti was at Spelman when I was at Morehouse, and we've stayed in touch ever since. She's one of the funniest people I know. During one of our many phone conversations, Patti hipped me to *the mo' better*, and I've used it ever since. Whether the title *Mo' Better Blues* lives up to the catchy *She's Gotta Have It*, *School Daze*, and the reigning champ, *Do the Right Thing*, remains to be seen.

The title of a film is an all-important marketing tool. It's the first thing people hear and see. A good title is a plus, but it's no substitute for a good film. The new Spike Lee joint will be called *Jungle Fever*. This time, the title was suggested by Lisa Jones. Based on the title, I wouldn't mind paying $7.50 to see the film myself.

Besides Denzel Washington, I wrote the first draft of *Mo' Better Blues* with a few other people in mind. I knew my sister Joie would be Indigo, the woman Bleek eventually marries. I knew Bill Nunn would be Bottom Hammer, Bleek's bass player. Buterbean, "Beneath the Underdog" 's resident comedian, was always Robin Harris. I wrote the role of Giant, Bleek's manager, for myself.

I've worked with people like Giant before. They mean well but they're incompetent. Whatever they do, they just get it wrong. Bleek grew up with Giant; they're best friends. Everybody in the movie tells Bleek that Giant is a terrible manager. Bleek would have fired him long ago, but loyalty prevents him. It's this allegiance to Giant, despite his compulsive gambling, that puts an end to Bleek's playing days. He goes to the mat for Giant, and gets his mouth fucked up in the process.

I wrote the role of Big Stop, Bleek's father, for Ossie Davis. Ossie was unable to do it, as he was scheduled to shoot a TV show with Burt Reynolds during our production period. Dick Anthony Williams did a fine job and was able to play both the old and young Big Stop. We didn't cast Dick until a few days before we needed him on camera. Luckily Denzel and Dick had worked together before, which made up for the lack of rehearsal time.

I read in the paper back in '89 that the father of New York Knicks forward Kenny Walker died. The article talked about how much his father meant to him. He was a big man from a little town in Georgia, and his nickname was Big Stop. The name just stuck in my head. I collect names for characters. Names are valuable; they can be your first source of insight into a character. Bleek's father got the name Big Stop when he played baseball in the Negro leagues. Big Stop calls his wife, Lillian, by the pet name Gem, which my father called my mother.

Often the parent who is the disciplinarian of a family is not as liked by the children as the other parent, who is perceived as the nice guy. When I was young, my mother was the heavy of our family and my father was nice guy. I wrote this into *Mo' Better Blues*. Bleek's mother, played by Abbey Lincoln, sets down the law. If things were left up to Big Stop, young Bleek would be out running the streets whenever he felt like it.

I gave the guys in the band nicknames to match the instruments they play: Rhythm Jones is a drummer, Bottom Hammer is a bass player, and Left Hand Lacey is a piano player. Saxophonist Shadow Henderson's name says he's in the background, but his personality says, "I should be out front." I like traditionally male names for women, so I gave the name Clarke to Bleek's other female friend. If I could rename Indigo now I would. Sometimes a name can be too much on the mark.

Indigo is a schoolteacher and Clarke is an aspiring singer. In the first draft, Clarke couldn't sing, but I realized that if Clarke had real talent, she would be a stronger character, and it would make a stronger point at the end of the film. Bleek only listens to his own music. He doesn't recognize Clarke's talent until it's too late. Not only does Clarke leave him for Shadow, but she becomes a big star, and Bleek can't even play anymore.

I was concerned while writing the script not to position the characters of Indigo and Clarke as good woman versus bad woman. I knew that casting was crucial, and that the women I cast would be far away from either stereotype. I was also concerned about skin complexion, knowing how divisive it has been to Black people. Early on, I intended to cast two brown-skinned women for the roles, thinking that this was my safest choice. If Bleek left a brown-skinned Clarke for a light-skinned Indigo, someone was bound to think I was making a statement about color. Or, God forbid, if both actresses had been light-skinned, sisters would have had my head. In the end, talent won out: Cynda Williams was Clarke, light-skinned or not, just as Joie Lee was Indigo, brown-skinned or not.

Mo' Better Blues went through two drafts. A few scenes were revised after the second draft and a few were added. Some of the added scenes were suggested by actors. I wrote in an additional scene to show Shadow courting Clarke. It was Cynda's suggestion that Clarke work at the jazz section of Tower Records, so I staged the scene there. We were able to secure Tower Records' Greenwich Village store as our location.

The songwriter Donald Fagen, formerly of the group Steely Dan, wrote a song for *Do the Right Thing* that I wasn't able to squeeze onto the soundtrack. In the first draft of *Mo' Better Blues* I had a scene in a recording studio with Donald Fagen and the singer Sade. Bleek is offered a job doing studio work on Sade's new single, produced by Fagen, but being the jazz purist that he is, he turns it down. Shadow takes the gig in his place. Sade didn't want to do the song, so I ended up cutting the scene altogether.

The first draft of a script is a sketch for me. I don't get the full story all at once. By the second draft, I know much more about the characters, and I can start filling in the blanks. For instance, I love films that complete a full circle. I decided early to begin *Mo' Better Blues* with young Bleek practicing his horn. It didn't come to me until much later, though, to end with Bleek's son Miles practicing his horn. During rehearsal period, someone (I forget who) suggested that I use the same actor, Zakee Howze, as the young Bleek and the young Miles.

I didn't feel as strong about the first draft of *Mo' Better Blues* as I did about *Do the Right Thing*. It surprised me that the first people who read the script liked it as much as they did. In one sense, the script seemed more conventional than any of my other films. I knew, though, that the way we shot the film would be anything but conventional. That's what makes Martin Scorsese such a great filmmaker. Read the script to any of his films, then go see the movie. It's not the words on the page that make his films so compelling, but how he chooses to illustrate them. *Raging Bull* is a prime example of this: good script, but masterpiece film.

I bought a bunch of photography books on jazz during preproduction to help me think about the images I wanted to bring to the screen. This is something I always do before I shoot, go through picture books and magazines, see movies. It helps me piece together the look of the film, then I bounce my ideas off Ernest, and vice versa. For all but two weeks of our preproduction period, Ernest was in Curaçao shooting a film for Felix deRoy, a classmate of ours from film school. Ernest and I kept in touch by fax machine. (I sent him sketches of the set and revisions of the script.) However, the look of the film didn't crystallize in our minds until almost two weeks into shooting. One thing we were sure about all along: We didn't want to shoot the entire movie in a dark, smoky hole-in-the-wall jazz club. There was going to be room to breathe in this film.

Despite the success of *Do the Right Thing*, we had long, drawn-out negotiations with Universal Pictures over the budget for this film. I didn't want to accept a budget that was lower than that of any of my previous films, or an inadequate, "token" raise. We went in asking for $11.5 million and came out with ten million bananas, my largest budget to date.

With this budget, we were able to shoot for ten weeks, instead of the eight we had on *Do the Right Thing*, and I gave the cast and crew a well-earned raise. We deserved to have that much money, if not more. *Do the Right Thing* made $28 million. In fact, all my films have made money.

At one point in the talks, Universal wanted to cut us a "tie-in" deal. If they could project that *Do the Right Thing* would make more than $30 million by a certain date, then we'd get more money for *Mo' Better Blues*. I thought we were being jerked. Not only had *Do the Right Thing* held its own at the box office, but it was the most critically successful film released by Universal in years. We were going to walk. We sent scripts to Orion, Paramount, and Geffen, but Universal came through with a compromise. I'm glad things worked out. We've had a good relationship with Universal so far and I didn't want to sever it.

Universal liked the script, but Big Cheese Tom Pollock was leery of the jazz milieu. He used the low grosses of *Bird* and *Round Midnight* as bargaining chips in our budget negotiations. But once the people at Universal started to see dailies of *Mo' Better Blues*, all the comparisons with low-grossing jazz films stopped. They were pleased with what they were seeing, whenever we sent them footage, which wasn't often. More important, they saw the film as a potential money-maker. They haven't mentioned *Bird* or *Round Midnight* since.

Denzel Washington as Bleek.

▼

The trumpet never left his hand for two months before we started to shoot: Denzel was great. I had no problems

with him whatsoever. He was willing to do, or at least try, whatever I suggested. I do think it's been hard on

him to hold his ego in check. Not to come down on Denzel, but when you're a Hollywood star, you're usually

catered to hand and foot. We didn't pamper him, but we did welcome him with open arms. And I'm sure he

felt good working with so many talented Black people, behind and in front of the camera.

▼

The Bleek Quintet and manager Giant.

Beauty pose courtesy of my brother, David Lee. David has been the still photographer on all my feature films.

His stills are featured in the montage of Brooklyn scenes that begins *She's Gotta Have It.* David started messing

around with cameras at Yale and he's been at it ever since. Another member of the talented Lee clan.

▼

Wesley Snipes as Shadow Henderson: "I have worked with actors who are less, quote unquote, talented, and actors who are less trained than I am. Especially White actors. If I was a young White guy doing the films that I've done, being featured in the co-starring roles that I've had, I would be making a million easy. Sometimes it bothers me, but I don't trip on it because that's the nature of this society. What it amounts to is this: I have to work harder. I have to be not only twice as good, but thrice as good, so that it's unequivocal, you can't deny it. The up side is, I'll never have to say that anyone did shit for me, because I worked for it."—WESLEY SNIPES

▼

THE
MO'
BETTER

Giancarlo Esposito had ten million props for his character, Left Hand Lacey: I was in film school when I first saw Giancarlo perform. He was in Charles Fuller's play *Zooman and the Sign.* I went backstage after the show and told him, "One day, I'd like to work with you." And we have: He was Big Brother Almighty in *School Daze,* Buggin' Out in *Do the Right Thing,* and Left Hand Lacey in *Mo' Better Blues.*

▼

Jeff Watts as Rhythm Jones: "Branford Marsalis told me in early '89 that Spike wanted me to read for the part. I never heard from Spike, so I guess he changed his mind and decided to use an experienced actor, but give him drum lessons. Then I heard that Spike had gone back to pursuing a real drummer. He held auditions in New York, and a half-dozen drummers came, but none of them could act. Again, he didn't ask me. He even went to Chicago and saw more drummers, but none of them could act either. Branford's band happened to be playing in Chicago at that time, and Spike came down to our gig. He told Branford and pianist Kenny Kirkland that he still couldn't find a drummer. Of course they wanted to know why he hadn't approached me. So, in a great feat of wisdom, Spike finally came to the right man! No, I'm just playing! He asked me to read for the part and I got it. I was very fortunate."—JEFF WATTS

▼

Bill Nunn as Bottom Hammer: Second to Nunn, old reliable. I saw Bill do plays at school, he went to Morehouse too. I'll use actors like Bill and Giancarlo again and again, not only because they're fine actors, but because they're versatile and they don't repeat themselves. To this day, people don't realize that the same guy who played Grady in *School Daze* was also Radio Raheem in *Do the Right Thing*.

▼

Joie Lee as Indigo: "I did a lot of thinking about the color indigo. I even went to a paint store to pick up a color wheel so I could study the color and the related shades of blue. I thought about the significance of the color blue. There is the blues, of course, and all the things that are colored blue, like the sky and ocean. So that's where I started from: What color is indigo?"—JOIE LEE

Two women and a horn.

▼

Cynda Williams as Clarke: "I knew the day I saw Cynda that she would be Clarke, I had a gut feeling. People ask me how I know if an actor is right for a role. I can never put it into words, I just *know.* Cynda was very nervous, and her first reading was mediocre. But I saw something more in her, so I had her sing. When she sang, she relaxed, so I had her read again. This reading was a lot better than the first. I gave her directions, and she was able to take them. I was pleased.

"I told Spike that I had met somebody I was really excited about, but he didn't meet her right away. When he did, I thought he would be much more taken with her. Spike usually gets excited when he feels he's found the right person. He didn't do that with Cynda, he just closed the door and sat down. I asked him right away what he thought. He seemed a bit indifferent. I said, 'She's gonna be Clarke, watch.'

"More than anything, he was concerned about the chemistry between Clarke and Bleek; it had to be hot. Spike wanted to involve Denzel in casting the role of Clarke. He asked that I bring Cynda back a couple of times to read with Denzel and Wesley, but I knew from day one."—ROBI REED, CASTING DIRECTOR

▼

Indigo and Bleek happily married forever after and all that stuff: "I saw *Glory* a month after we wrapped on *Mo' Better Blues*. I cried watching that film. Just seeing Denzel out there moved me. I had forgotten what a powerful actor he is. Before we met, the only film I had seen him in was *A Soldier's Story*. I hadn't seen any of his other work.

"When I saw Denzel in *Glory*, I experienced Denzel-the-heartthrob for the first time, which was funny because I had never thought of him that way before. People came up to me all the time during the shoot, 'You're acting with Denzel, ohhh! You're gonna do a love scene with him? Awhhh!' I never could understand it. But *Glory* made me so proud of Denzel. Oh my God, I almost felt like I was watching my husband. It really did feel that way, I was so proud. I must congratulate him. It was a great performance."—JOIE LEE

▼

I'll settle for some of dat Mo' Better cuz ya know da Mo' Better makes it Mo' Better: ''The men on the set were very chauvinistic.

My intelligence was questioned time and time again. I don't think he realized it, but Spike even did it a couple of times. Before I

got the role, he was testing me, asking me questions like 'Do you know who Marcus Garvey is?' Finally I said, 'Spike, stop testing

me. If you were my teacher in a Black history class, it would be different.' ''—CYNDA WILLIAMS

▼

"Denzel and Wesley were interesting to watch. They're both extremely talented, but they come at it in a different way. Denzel is like a surgeon: precise, thought-out, meticulous. Wesley is more of a raw talent. He's got shitloads of talent, but he still works hard at his craft."—BILL NUNN

▼

In rehearsal: "I don't think Denzel knew much about Wesley before this film. When he heard that Wesley was playing Shadow, he began to investigate. He asked people, 'Who is this Wesley Snipes?' and all the feedback was positive. But I don't think he knew what Wesley was capable of until the full-cast read-through of the script that took place during the first week of rehearsals. There was a moment when Wesley delivered a line, and Denzel just stopped. He was looking at his script, but he turned and looked over at Wesley, who was sitting a few chairs down. I think it started to sink in then—'I really have an actor here, I have someone to work off of.' "—ROBI REED

"We started off with don'ts. We didn't want the film to look dark like *Bird*. We didn't want to focus on the self-destructiveness of jazz musicians, like White filmmakers had done in the past. We knew we were going to be the first filmmakers in a while to look at jazz from a Black perspective. And the conflict of our film centered around musicians and their personal relationships. In particular, a musician who loses sight of others because of his devotion to the music.

"I felt that the film called for a fluid camera style. We wanted to create visual rhythms that approximated the audio rhythms of jazz, which is something we've experimented with in all of our films. Because this is a love story, I knew the lighting had to be softer, more romantic. *Do the Right Thing* was about heat and tension, so I used hot light and hard light. *Mo' Better Blues* had to be cool like jazz—passionate, but also aloof. Often in the same scene, I would include light at opposite ends of the spectrum: warm light—the oranges and yellows —and cooler lights—the blues."—ERNEST DICKERSON

▼

Setting up a shot with camera operator John Newby: Unlike *Do the Right Thing,* Ernest and I didn't nail the style and look of *Mo' Better Blues* until the second or third week of shooting. Ernest calls it romantic. I don't know if I would use that term, but it is something along that line. Whatever you call the style, it took us a while to find it. This was especially true for me, as far as directing the camera.

If the script reads "and then they make love," there's a lot of work a director must do to get that moment on screen. It's not the best strategy to go to the set and decide at the last minute how to realize a scene. But some of the best stuff we did in this film came the morning of the shoot.

▼

Dark Gable: "When Denzel came in for his first fitting, I showed him the color palette I prepared for his character. Bleek would wear rich tones in the beginning of the film. After his breakdown, and throughout the montage sequence, we would see him in more muted tones.

"When Denzel came back for a second fitting, I had him try on every outfit in the order of the script. Of course, there were things that he liked and things that he didn't like, so we had more fittings during the rehearsal period. The costume department was two floors below the rehearsal space, and each time Denzel came down for a fitting, he had his trumpet and he was in character. I'd get a shirt on him and he'd sit down with that trumpet and start blowing. And I'd say, 'Okay, let's get the pants on.' He'd put the pants on and he'd sit down and blow some more. It would take twenty minutes for him to try a suit on. And because he was discovering who Bleek was, he became very sensitive to the character's likes and dislikes."—RUTHE CARTER, COSTUME DESIGNER

▼

Rubén Blades as Petey the Bookie: "I bought this dice changer at an antique fair some time ago. On one side it has the mask of humor, on the other, the mask of tragedy. Towards the end of the film, I turned to the sad face to show how the dice are rolling for Giant."—RUBÉN BLADES

▼

Bouncers Eggy and Born Knowledge (Charles Murphy and Steve White) in front of "Beneath the Underdog." I named the club after the Charles Mingus autobiography.

▼

Giancarlo Esposito tickling the 88's: "Denzel's a method actor. What 'method acting' means to me is when an actor just *becomes* a character, whether it's in rehearsal or on the set. Denzel, I would notice, would go off alone and go through whatever process he had to go through to become Bleek. Then he would be Bleek for the rest of the day, and would answer you like Bleek would answer you. Giancarlo is the extreme of this. Once he became Left Hand Lacey, there was no turning him off, period!"—ROBI REED

▼

Two broken digits: Things just never work out right for Giant, no matter what he does, he's got bad luck. Associating yourself with people like him can be dangerous. It's Bleek's loyalty to Giant that destroys his music career. On the other hand, it might be what saves Bleek in the end. Out of the devastation that comes from not being able to play professionally, he finds himself. And he finds that he can love and be loved. I really don't think Bleek could have been a happily married family man if it weren't for the accident.

▼

On tenor and soprano, Shadow Henderson: "You don't come to a Spike Lee joint without something as an actor. If you're expecting to be coached into your character, forget it, it's not gonna happen. Spike's carrying enough hats as it is. You have to be very confident as an actor, because he's gonna give you free rein. And if you've done your homework, when you come to the set, you'll come up with something. Your performance is not gonna be ambivalent, you'll make definitive choices. And growing as an actor is about learning to stand on your own two feet."—WESLEY SNIPES

▼

The ritual: We wanted to show how hard Bleek works at his music, so we filmed a montage of Bleek practicing his horn. We had Denzel sit on a dolly (a mount that allows the camera to move during filming) and moved it in circles, so he appears to be revolving around the room. There's a light on him, but the background is dark. When Clarke stops by unexpectedly and rings his buzzer, the dolly stops, the lights go down on him, and the lights come up in the background, as if he has snapped out of his trance.

We did a similar shot of Clarke and Bleek kissing passionately as the room appears to spin around. We had Denzel and Cynda sit together on the dolly seat, and rotated the dolly as the camera tracked with them. Nasty!

▾

Photo session: "For Bleek, every moment of his life is mapped out. He can only give so much to other people. He's afraid that someone, mainly one of his woman friends, will take away his God-given talent. What he fails to understand is that if it's God-given, then nobody can take it from you. It's there for you to use, to express, and you give thanks. It doesn't come from you, it comes through you. It's wonderful to have that kind of talent in one's life, but it's almost blasphemous not to share it."—JOIE LEE

▼

Big yams!: "Being a light-skinned Black woman has not landed me more roles as an actress. Casting agents say they want women who are 'pure Black.' Just what is that?

"I'm not a mulatto, I'm Black. My mother is White, but that has no bearing on my experience. I accept my mother for who she is and I accept that part of my bloodline, but it's not the leading force in my life. This has a lot to do with how I was raised, because I was raised as a Black woman. My parents have always said, you'll never be half and half. People will never look at you through those eyes. They will always look at you as a Black woman, period. You're Black, so love it, accept it, and want to be it."

—CYNDA WILLIAMS

▼

Giant and Bleek watch Clarke sing "Harlem Blues."

▼

The montage sequence: "Spike's been my older brother and I've been his younger sister for twenty-seven years, and that's bound to carry over into our professional relationship. I would yell at Spike, 'I'm not disagreeing with you as your sniveling younger sister, I'm disagreeing with you as an actress. And you're not talking to me as a director, you're talking to me as my older brother.' And he would yell back, 'No, I'm not!' And then an argument would ensue. We went at it all the time in rehearsals. Denzel just sat back and laughed at us."

—JOIE LEE

Cynda looks like a million bucks here. Jesus Christ. Great day in the mornin'!: "When I saw *School Daze* back home in Indiana, I said to myself, 'I can do this.' When I moved to New York City, I would walk down the street thinking, what if Spike Lee came up to me right now, what would I say to him? Naturally, I was nervous when I got my chance to audition for him just eight months after I moved to the city.

"Spike can give the most intimidating looks at times, und he had one on his face during my audition. I had never tried out for a film before, only for commercials and plays, so I didn't know there was a difference. Robi had a video camera set up, and I delivered my lines directly into the camera, like one would do for a commercial. After my reading, Spike said, 'That was great, but don't ever look at the camera.' I could have shot myself in the head."—CYNDA WILLIAMS

▼

The Dracula love scene. Let me bite your neck: "There was a lot of playfulness between Bleek and Indigo. We didn't anticipate this, it just happened. Like in the scene where Bleek comes to visit Indigo after a gig. They're about to kiss and he descends on her like Count Dracula. Spike said to think about the old black-and-white vampire movies and how the woman would turn and toss to avoid the vampire's fangs. Actually, I did it first, then Spike said, 'Yeah, yeah, I like that, do it more.' It definitely wasn't scripted. When I saw the dailies, it occurred to me that this was the first time I had seen such playful affection between a Black couple on a film."

—JOIE LEE

▾

Is this a real-looking band or what? (The Bleek Quintet, minus Left Hand Lacey): "One night after rehearsal,

the guys in the band went out to a restaurant in the Village. We had some margaritas, some shrimp, and we

were talking jazz. Really, we were making it all up, like 'Yeah, man, Monk was this, Monk was that, blah,

blah, blah.' Those margaritas started to kick in.

"Bill had passes to the 'Paradise Club,' so we went there. I had both saxophones, soprano and tenor, and

Denzel had his trumpet. We hung out by ourselves in the back of the club playing our horns and carrying on.

We were seriously off-key. It was a riot. I went to the bathroom and when I came back, the fellas were

surrounded by a posse of women saying things like 'Are you guys really musicians?'

" 'Yeah, baby, yeah, we play.'

" 'What's the name of the band?'

" 'The Bleek Quartet. We've been traveling around Europe. We just got back.' " —WESLEY SNIPES

▼

I kept all of Giant's clothes. Too clean!: I read a review of one of my films that said I had mastered the deadpan. Giant is definitely not in that vein. He's nothing *but* loud. Being loud is probably his way of compensating for being small in stature. Though it's never mentioned in the dialogue, no one gave him the nickname Giant; he gave it to himself. To have Giant's clothes match his personality, I asked Ruthe to make sure they fit big. He's just a flamboyant character—the exaggerated walk, the hats, the flashy watch, all that stuff.

▼

"Mo' Better Blues was such a relaxing shoot, it was difficult. Ordinarily I'm able to separate myself, or alienate myself, in some way from the people I'm working with on a film. It works for me as an actor, because I can concentrate on the work alone. It was harder to do that on this film, because when you do that to your own, they think you have an attitude. I'm sure folks on the set sometimes said, 'Oh, he's Hollywood, he's got an attitude.' All I was trying to do was concentrate on the work.

"But it was a pleasure, overall, easily the most enjoyable film I've done yet. It's sad to hear people ask, 'How was working with Spike?' When I tell them it was great, they say, 'Really?' I say, 'Yeah. What do you mean *really?*' Our people. Our people."—DENZEL WASHINGTON

▼

mo'
B E T T E R
PRODUCTION
N O T E S

Mo' Better Blues was shot in Brooklyn and Manhattan and on a soundstage in Long Island City, Queens, from September 24 to December 1, 1989.

WEEK ONE: SEPTEMBER 25-29, 1989

We had a difficult first day of shooting. It reminded me of day one of *Do the Right Thing*. There was only one shot to complete, but it involved a complicated camera move, as well as extras and dialogue for the main actors. My character, Mookie, comes down the steps of his house, says "Hell no" to Jehovah's Witnesses selling newspapers at his doorstep, walks down the block, then stops to talk to Mother Sister, the eyes and ears of the community, before heading to work at Sal's Famous Pizzeria. We were able to cover all the action in one shot by using a crane, but it took many takes to get it right.

Our first shot of *Mo' Better Blues* happened to be the opening shot of the movie. The film was shot out of sequence, as most are. The only reason we scheduled the opening scene on the first day was to knock it off while the weather was still warm. We were fortunate enough to have an extended Indian summer, which allowed us to do all the exteriors during the first two weeks as scheduled. We were rained out one day, but moved quickly to an interior scene (reserved as a "cover set" for these occasions), so the day wasn't wasted.

For this first shot we used a Louma crane. It begins with the camera pointing straight up at the trees, holds for five seconds (long enough to burn in the title "Brooklyn 1969"), then we crane down a block of vintage brownstones. Four kids come down the block. The camera follows them up to Bleek's stoop as they yell for him to come out of the house and play. We did thirteen takes. Again, it was a matter of choreographing the movement of the crane, the kids, the picture cars (cars used as props), and the extras playing passersby.

We were on location in the Brooklyn community of Park Slope. It wasn't necessary to do any construction or set dressing on the block to date it twenty years in the past. We used period cars and dressed extras in period costume, but that was it. This was my second experience filming a period scene. The first was for "No One in the World," a video for Anita Baker set in the 1940s, which we shot at Harlem's Apollo Theater in 1987.

Five weeks before we filmed this scene I asked the kids to start growing their hair to Afro length. This proved not to be enough time, so we had resort to Afro wigs. I was concerned that the wigs would look fake, but they were our only alternative. Chris Skeffrey, the young actor with the crossed eyes who plays Louis, is the only kid without a wig. He had a Jheri curl at the time, but once we washed out the activator and gave him the once-over with an Afro pick, you couldn't tell the difference.

We auditioned tons of kids for the roles of young Bleek and his friends. Finding a good child actor is even harder than finding an adult. Your typical child actor is very affected. Parents stick them in commercial classes where they learn to smile and cry on cue. They're too cutesy for me. Chris' eyes gave him an offbeat look; he's also intelligent and he took directions well. Another one of young Bleek's friends is called Joe in the script. Ruthe Carter, our costume designer, dressed Raymond Thomas, the young actor we cast as Joe, in a baseball cap and glasses. He looked so much like me that Ruthe suggested that I change the role of Joe to the young Giant, which I did.

Raymond had a funny audition. There was some cursing in the kids' scenes. I asked every kid who auditioned for us to curse to make sure he felt comfortable with it. Raymond refused to at first, saying his mother was right outside the door. Robi told him that cursing under these circumstances was different because he was acting, and it was the character speaking, not him. Raymond looked around like he was checking on his mother, then yelled, "Bleek, you fucking bum!" Robi and I fell out laughing. I used his line in the movie.

Zakee Howze, who played young Bleek and young Miles, did a fine job. Looking at his performance in dailies, I knew that the audience would know exactly why Bleek does everything that he does the rest of the film, just by what Zakee establishes in the first three minutes. But working with little kids, no matter how good they are, is always a trying experience. Their attention spans are short and they tire easily. If they don't get it right on the first take, especially if it's a lengthy shot, you're in for trouble. The quality of their performances tends to deteriorate take by take.

That first day, after we did the involved shot with the crane descending from the trees, we set up for close-ups of young Bleek. The other kids were finished for the day, and I took Zakee back to the trailer to go over his lines. All of a sudden he started to cry, "I wanna go, I wanna go home." I told him if he stopped bawling and did a few good takes, I'd give him ten dollars. Zakee shut up right away, wiped away his tears, and asked me not to tell anyone he was crying. Sure enough, he went back to the set and busted it out. I promised him if he did as well the next day, I'd give him another ten. Candy just doesn't work anymore.

The issue of *Newsweek* with my picture on the cover (the feature story was on American innovators) hit the stands on our first day of production. Neighborhood folks stopped me on the set throughout the day to ask me to sign copies. Other interesting coincidences: The Saturday before our first day of shooting was John Coltrane's birthday. The first day of production on *Do the Right Thing* was Nelson Mandela's birthday. Both *Do the Right Thing* and *She's Gotta Have It* were accepted to the Cannes Film Festival on my birthday, March 20. I must be doing something right.

The next day we shot the continuation of the first scene, which takes place in the interior of the Gilliam family's brownstone. Young Bleek is chastised by his mother for wanting to play with his friends instead of practicing his trumpet. As Mrs. Gilliam (or Gem, as Big Stop calls her), Abbey Lincoln worked both days. Abbey is known primarily as a jazz singer, though she's played some wonderful roles as an actress. I loved her in *Nothing but a Man* and *For the Love of Ivy*—it's a shame she doesn't have the opportunity to work more in films.

Abbey was once married to the drummer Max Roach. Ernest told me that he wanted to ask her what life with a jazz pioneer like Max was like, but he thought better of it. I wanted to do the same, but also held my tongue. I gave Abbey a copy of Brian Lanker's book *I Dream a World: Portraits of Black Women Who Changed America* when she wrapped on the second day, which was her last day of shooting. I remember Abbey in the full-cast read-through on the first day of rehearsals. She sat by herself in a corner. I think she was upset that she didn't have a larger role. I talked to her afterward and did my best to express how important the part was, no matter how small. Abbey could have turned us down, even that late in the game, but she worked her two days without complaint.

Bleek's father, Big Stop, appears in that scene also. He wrenches himself away from a ball game on TV to console young Bleek about not being allowed out to play. The role, originally written for Ossie Davis, was filled by veteran actor Dick Anthony Williams. I remember seeing Dick in Bill Gunn's play *The Black Picture Show* at New York's Public Theater. I was in high school at the time. Dick was also in *Serpico* with Al Pacino.

We literally had three days to cast the role of Big Stop once Ossie pulled out. We were in a panic. It seemed like every actor we contacted—Morgan Freeman, Danny Glover, Bill Cobb—wasn't available. We were lucky to get Dick to work on such little notice. He flew into New York from California on a Saturday, and we shot his first scene on a Tuesday. As soon as he got in, I rehearsed with him and Denzel for three hours.

Days three and four we shot the exteriors of Bleek's loft, the scenes with Bleek and Big Stop playing catch. We were on location in Brooklyn Heights near the waterfront. Traffic and noise were killers. There was noise from all directions— our sound man even picked up a work crew in the middle of the Brooklyn Bridge, practically a quarter of a mile away.

Day four was Joie's first day. She didn't have much to do. She comes down the front steps to Bleek's place, kisses Big Stop and Bleek, then rushes off to school. Joie and I had our share of run-ins during the shoot. Her approach to acting is an intellectual one. This is not a criticism. As a director, I accept any actor's approach as long as the result is a performance that I'm satisfied with. There's a scene where Indigo is sitting on her stoop waiting for Bleek. Joie asked why Indigo would wait on the stoop and not in the house. I wanted to start the scene outside, then bring it inside—there was no other reason than that. This didn't make sense to Joie, but she went along with what I asked.

Also on day four, we stole some shots for the *Love Supreme* montage. In pre-production we prepared ourselves to grab shots for the montage whenever the opportunity presented itself. The appropriate costumes were always standing by in the wardrobe truck. So after finishing the work schedule for day four, we filmed Denzel and Joie near the East River.

On Friday, Rubén Blades and I did a scene that takes place in Giant's crib. The location we used was an empty apartment in Brooklyn Heights that our production designer, Wynn Thomas, had completely furnished and set-dressed.

I met Rubén when I asked him to do a song for *Do the Right Thing*. (It's called "Tú y Yo." You hear it in the "battle of the boom boxes" scene between the Puerto Rican guys and Radio Raheem.) I'm a fan of Rubén's music and his acting. I liked him in *Crossover Dreams* and Robert Redford's *Milagro Beanfield War*. Though people may think of Rubén as a musician who moonlights as an actor, as of '89 he had nine films under his belt. I'm sure he's involved in more as of this writing.

I think Rubén gives a great performance as Giant's bookie, Petey. At first I was leery of offering a small roll like Petey to Rubén, but he was enthusiastic about working with me. The role was originally not on camera. Petey was supposed to appear as a voice-over in a series of phone conversations with Giant, which was lazy filmmaking on my part. By the second draft, I made Petey an on-screen character.

People ask how the idea for Giant as a gambler came to be. I guess the Pete Rose scandal had something to do with it since it was in the news while I was writing the script. For those who don't know, the star baseball player turned manager was accused of betting on baseball. The scene with Giant and Petey that takes place in Giant's apartment starts on a couple of insert shots (shots that are taken outside of the main action of a scene) of various items in the room, ending with a poster of Pete Rose. The camera holds on Rose, then I walk into the frame and we follow me to the table where Rubén is sitting.

On the set the morning we shot in Giant's apartment, I had a little revelation. The scene previous to this one ends with Clarke biting Bleek's lip. Bleek's last line is "I make my living with my lips." The set dressers had included a small statue of a Black woman on the set of Giant's pad, which kept catching my eye. I got the idea to begin the scene with an extreme close-up of the statue's lips. It's a nice transition from Bleek's last line to the statue. Lips are a recurring image in this film. Bleek is always touching his lips and doctoring them with lip balm. Of course, in the end, it's a damaged lip that alters his life.

This first week was the smoothest I've ever had on a film shoot. Day one was our longest; the other four days we wrapped by or before five o'clock in the afternoon, after starting at seven in the morning. I knew I had long hours and some whip-cracking to do in the weeks to come, but it was a pleasant start. The crew was getting along fine. We had a good group of professionals and many young, hungry interns. All but two of the department heads are Black, including Ernest, the director of photography; Wynn, the production designer; Ruthe, the costume designer; Charles Houston, the gaffer; and Randy Fletcher, the assistant director. I often wondered about the White crew members joining us for the first time on this project. In this lily-white industry, working with so many Black people was undoubtedly a new experience for them.

WEEK TWO: OCTOBER 2-6, 1989

We were scheduled to shoot an exterior scene in Prospect Park on Monday. When I woke up at 5:30 A.M. it was raining. On day shoots our camera, grip, and electric trucks leave for a location before the crack of dawn, so it was too late to give the drivers other directions. It made sense for everybody to meet at the park, even though we had to move to another location. I announced the cover set when the entire crew was assembled at the park. We made a full-company move from Brooklyn to midtown Manhattan, the location of Shadow's apartment.

This was the first day of shooting for Shadow, played by Wesley Snipes. I've been a fan of Wesley's work for a while. I first saw him in "Bad," the Michael Jackson video directed by Martin Scorsese. He was also in *Wildcats* with Goldie Hawn and a low-budget film called *Streets of Gold*. I offered him the role of Ahmad in *Do the Right Thing*, but he turned me down to do *Major League* with Charlie Sheen, a good move on his part. Wesley did do a couple days of looping (rerecording dialogue during postproduction) for *Do the Right Thing*. Originally I had Gregory Hines in mind for the role of Shadow, but he turned me down. I'm extremely pleased with Wesley's performance in the film. He gives Denzel, the more experienced actor, a run for his money.

We shot three scenes at Shadow's apartment. The first was Giant returning a rare Charlie Parker album borrowed by Bleek, then the funny scene that follows of Shadow asking Giant to smell his sheets. I envisioned shooting more coverage of the sheets scene, but we did it in one setup (the angle at which the camera is placed). The shot ends with Shadow throwing a pillowcase over the camera lens, which makes for a nice transition to the scene that follows, Bleek and Clarke in bed.

Our final shot of the day was Bleek's imaginary point of view of Shadow and Clarke boning on the terrace of Shadow's apartment. This was done with a handheld camera. The shot begins in the living room, where you see Clarke's clothes on the floor. Then we had the camera operator run from the living room onto the terrace, where Shadow and Clarke are simulating the mo' better thirty-nine floors above the street.

The weather cleared up on Tuesday. We went back outside, this time to Brooklyn Heights. Bleek and Giant return from Prospect Park on the bikes, then go their separate ways. I'm biking down the street when the hoods Rod and Madlock, played by Leonard Thomas and Sam Jackson, trip me with their car door.

This was my first stunt scene. I had the option of using a stunt person, but ruled against it. I'm recognizable enough for audiences to spot the fake. Once I got over the fear of that first jump, I was fine. The grip department built a ramp up to the car door. I had to run up the ramp, dive over the door, and land on a mattress. A rig was set up for the bike as well. When I jumped over the car door, the grips would pull the bike rig, sending the bike flying along with me. We did many takes at various speeds to give us options in the editing room.

The assistant director, Randy Fletcher, and the stunt coordinator, Jeff Ward, saw that I took every precaution. The first time I went over I played possum as if I were hurt. Everyone rushed over. Actually, it was nothing to joke about. You do have to be careful with stunts.

Earlier in the day we had shot the scene that directly follows my stunt scene. The hoods take Giant for a ride and break his fingers. Leonard Thomas had the opportunity to show off an old football injury. There was damage to the joint of one of the fingers on his right hand. He's able to bend it as if it were rubber. Leonard used the finger to intimidate Giant.

Wednesday we shot Bleek and Giant riding bikes in Prospect Park, which we were rained out of on Monday. This was my first significant scene with Denzel. The camera rode on a truck stabilized to cut down on bumps and outfitted with a special camera rig. We did three different setups. First we rigged the camera from behind the truck, so it filmed Denzel and me straight on. Then, we had the camera rigged in front, so it captured us from behind. Finally, the camera was mounted on the side, to pick us up in profile.

We moved to the gazebo on the lake to shoot Bleek telling Giant he's not doing a good job as manager. The city obliged us by closing the park to traffic for the entire day. We still had to make way for joggers and bikers.

On Thursday we set up shop at Pluto's Restaurant, a Greek coffee shop on Myrtle Avenue in Brooklyn, my breakfast hangout during my film-school days. We didn't alter the shop in any way in terms of production design or set dressing. There was one thing: We moved a "fish on a bun" sign from the restaurant window and placed it more prominently in the scene.

Giant's bookie, Petey—Rubén Blades—takes his bets and issues him a warning about his debts. This was Rubén's last day. I was sorry to see him go. My main man and co-producer, Monty Ross, was an extra in the coffee shop. He sits down next to Giant at the counter. There's no business between us, but seeing us in this context should amuse those who know us well. Monty started out as an actor. He was the lead in *Joe's Bed-Stuy Barbershop: We Cut Heads*, my thesis project at New York University. He's spending his time behind the camera these days.

We begin the scene with an insert shot of two sunny-side-up eggs sizzling on the grill. We never got them perfectly round the way I wanted them. They were supposed to look like breasts, but it didn't work out.

We did a company move nearby to the location of Clarke's apartment to film Shadow and Clarke boning. Our location for Clarke's apartment was a landmark building in my neighborhood, Fort Greene, Brooklyn. Ironically, we chose the location not for the exterior, but for the oversize rooms that gave us space to do a long tracking shot. The shot begins on Shadow's sax in the living room and moves to the bedroom, where Shadow and Clarke are boning away. Along the way, we see photographs of Clarke's idols, Ella Fitzgerald, Dinah Washington, Sarah Vaughan, and Billie Holiday.

Cynda and Wesley shot both of their love scenes this week. In fact, Cynda's first two shooting days both involved love scenes. On *School Daze* and *Do the Right*

Thing, we saved the love scenes for last, so the actors could have as much time as possible to feel comfortable with each other. Our schedule on this film didn't allow me the luxury. We reserved the last three weeks of production to film the club scenes on a soundstage, and everything else we juggled around that.

There's no big deal to filming love scenes. They're mechanical in a sense. You move bodies around like mannequins. There's not much room for improvisation. I will say one thing about this particular scene: The dynamics between Wesley and Cynda were hot. She was very relaxed. I gave her my word that it would be tasteful. She discussed the nudity with her parents and grandparents, and they gave her their blessing.

This film marked a number of "firsts" for Cynda. It was her first time on camera, her first film, and her first love scene. Cynda was born in Chicago, but the family moved later to Muncie, Indiana. She majored in theater arts at Ball State University and moved to New York in January 1989.

Before *Do the Right Thing* was released, Cynda's grandmother had a dream that she would have a chance to work with me. Cynda heard about the auditions for *Mo' Better Blues*, came down without an appointment, and waited there until Robi would see her. Robi gave her a shot and loved her. I was in L.A. at the time, but Robi called me to rave about Cynda. I felt the same way when she came in again to read for me, but it was too early in our audition process to commit. I put Cynda on hold, but knew all along that she was the front-runner. I bought her a couple of Toni Morrison novels and even let her read the script before actually giving her the role.

In the auditions we had Cynda improvise, read from the script, sing, and just talk with us. She auditioned for me three times, then a final time with Denzel. Of the top three picks who read for Denzel, Cynda was his first choice. Denzel was helpful in these sessions. He made the actresses feel at ease, so they could do their best work possible.

Friday was our first night shoot. It's the only time in the film that we see the exterior of "Beneath the Underdog," so it was an important establishing shot. Our production design for this location was inspired by a photograph I saw in a book called *Jazz Giants*. It's a 1950s night shot of Manhattan's West 52nd Street, the jazz strip of the day. I showed Wynn the photo and he took it from there. He found a great location, the Cherry Lane Theatre on Commerce Street in Greenwich Village. The art department took two days to construct a facade for the theater and the adjacent buildings to create our version of West 52nd Street.

We covered the entire scene in one shot. The Louma crane starts high on the buildings, then cranes down to reveal the row of clubs and the long line in front of "Beneath the Underdog." When the camera gets to the end of the line. Giant starts walking across the street and almost gets hit by a cab. The cab drives off and the camera moves with Giant to the entrance of the "Underdog." The bouncers, Eggy and Born Knowledge, played by Charles Murphy and Steve White, prevent Giant from going through the front entrance. It was a complicated shot. We did eighteen takes before we were satisfied with it. We spent the rest of the evening doing pick-up shots to give the editor something to play with in the cutting room.

I visited the block only once during a location scout. I decided then to do the scene in one shot. Originally I wanted the camera to crane down on Giant tying his shoe in the middle of the street. Later on I had to ask myself, Why would a man tie his shoe in the middle of the street? I squashed that and instead had Giant walk out in front of a cab. It was better visually. After the first few takes, I remember Dustin Hoffman's famous line in *Midnight Cowboy*, "I'm walking here, I'm walking here," and decided to add it to the scene. The script supervisor questioned me about the line, assuming I didn't know the reference. That shit pissed me off.

You get to see Giant's exaggerated walk up close in this scene. I modeled it on the way super-cool guys walk, they lean to one side and swing their hands. Giant makes it his trademark by keeping his right shoulder higher than his left.

The "Beneath the Underdog" exterior was one of our "money shots." Night shoots generally cost more, but building the set, renting the crane, and hiring a large number of extras made this one of our most expensive shooting days.

At the end of the second week, I realized what a luxury shoot this had been so far. The length alone—we had eight weeks for *Do the Right Thing*, ten for *Mo' Better Blues*—allowed us to work at a more humane pace. We often pulled long days on *Do the Right Thing*. When we finished the scheduled scenes early, we would move on to the next day's work. That was a big advantage to shooting on one primary location. On *Mo' Better Blues*, when we finished our scheduled work we really had to call it a day. You want to avoid company moves as much as possible. They're a big hassle and cost you an arm and a leg.

WEEK THREE: OCTOBER 10–13, 1989

We were off Monday for the Columbus Day holiday. Tuesday we shot two-thirds of our first musical sequence, "M & N," written by my father. Great scene— unfortunately, it didn't make the final cut of the film.

MO'
BETTER
NOTES

I wanted to have a sequence that again showed the triangle, Bleek, Indigo, and Clarke, but showed it musically. I came up with the idea of tying the sequence to a song written by Bleek for Indigo's class. The sequence begins with Bleek practicing the song on his trumpet, cuts to a classroom where Indigo leads her third graders in the song, then cuts again to Clarke singing the same song in her voice lessons. We cut back and forth from location to location.

We shot the scene in a classroom of a local Brooklyn Catholic school. Again, this was a case where there was no need for set dressing. The location was fine as is. My father wanted to make "M & N" more of a big production number, with choreography and hats. I felt it was more believable unrehearsed.

Prior to the shoot, Joie and I had a big argument about the scene. She was adamant that a third-grade class wouldn't sing an alphabet song. I told her it didn't matter, Bleek wrote the song for her class and that was the important thing. Nobody in the movie theater was going to question why a third-grade class was singing about the alphabet.

"M & N" was our longest day up until that point. We were shooting with two cameras. Without the extra camera, we would have gone even longer.

Wednesday was a light day. In the morning we went to Tower Records in the Village to shoot the scene of Shadow courting Clarke, who works as a cashier in the jazz section. I wanted a 6:00 A.M. call, but had to change it to 7:00 A.M. We went late the previous night and had to make our twelve-hour turnaround—film union regulations mandate that there be a twelve-hour off time between shooting days. We were supposed to be out of Tower by 9:00 A.M., when the store opened, but they let us stay until we finished, at 10:30 A.M.

After Tower we went around the corner to Great Jones Street to do a long tracking shot of the band exiting Jones Diner and walking down the block. We set up more than four hundred feet of dolly track on the sidewalk. (The camera is mounted on the dolly. The camera operator also rides the dolly. The dolly is then pushed by grips down the track. The entire setup allows you to capture moving action in a smooth, continuous manner.) This scene also was cut from the film.

Before wrapping for the day, we moved to a third location, the Bleek Quintet's rehearsal space, and set our lights for the next day's shoot. While the crew set up, the band members ran through the musical number on board for the day ahead.

Our location for the rehearsal space was a photography studio with big bay windows. We filmed there all day—lots of moving camera shots, hand-held and on dolly. I was struck by the believability of the band members. Denzel and Wesley had the fingering down, and so did the other guys. They looked like real musicians.

Today was the first time the music coaches were on set. Every time we shot a musical sequence they were there, watching their pupils and making sure the fingering, mannerisms, and breathing were accurate, or at least believable. I did not want jazz critics like Stanley Crouch nitpicking about the realism of the music scenes. I can hear them now: "How could Spike Lee, son of a famous jazz musician, Bill Lee, present jazz music inaccurately, especially after he criticized Clint Eastwood's film?" Give me a break, guys!

Ruthe Carter had the chance to show off her talent on this film. Even in the rehearsal scene, the band is sharp. And the hats! Especially the hats! All the guys wanted to keep their costumes. At the end of production, we had a costume sale, and you know who was the first on line—the Bleek Quintet.

We had a great day on Friday, the most relaxed and enjoyable of the entire shoot. We had a twelve o'clock call because we went late the night before. In the morning, we shot some scenes from the montage. The first was Bleek and Indigo escorting the young Miles to his first day of kindergarten, which we shot in Brooklyn Heights. What we attempted to do with the montage scenes was give them a home-movie feel. We didn't rehearse the camera moves. If the shots were jerky and out of focus at times, it would work toward the overall look of the sequence.

After the montage shots, we made a company move nearby to the Brooklyn Bridge to get a shot of Indigo and Bleek walking across at sunset, known as "magic hour" in film terminology because it doesn't last long. After dinner we set up for our famous Louma-crane shot of Denzel playing trumpet on the bridge. We did two versions of this shot. One is a pensive moment after a gig. The other is right after both of Bleek's women have left him. It's a lonely moment, so I had Denzel put a mute on the trumpet. Only the lonely shot made the final cut of the film.

The song Bleek plays on the bridge is "Sing Soweto" by Terence Blanchard, Denzel's music coach. Terence was on the set that night and he kept saying, "Spike, when women see these shots, they'll go crazy." He was right. Denzel Washington, in a suit, playing trumpet alone on the Brooklyn Bridge, with the Manhattan skyline in the background. You can't get much sexier than that!

It was a warm Indian-summer night. There were a lot of people walking and riding bikes in the pedestrian lane. We were able to talk the city into letting us use golf carts to shuttle our equipment from the foot of the bridge to the middle, so the night went like clockwork.

The shoot was proceeding like a breeze. But I knew the last three weeks at the soundstage filming the club scenes would be hard knocks—music scenes, two hundred extras, smoke. Plain hard work!

WEEK FOUR: OCTOBER 16–20, 1989

Our location manager, Brent Owens, found us just the right spot to create Bleek's apartment—a spacious loft in Brooklyn Heights, with exposed beams and a perfect view of the Brooklyn Bridge and Manhattan skyline. On Monday we began two weeks of shooting there. The second will be a week of night shoots.

In the morning we shot Clarke interrupting Bleek's daily ritual of practicing the horn. I had Denzel lean against a pillar, another one of the location's architectural details that we were able to make use of. Clarke appears from behind the pillar. She whispers in Bleek's left ear, then his right. The camera dollies from side to side with her. The shot looked great in dailies. It worked out better than expected considering I thought it up on the spot.

You don't want to come on set unprepared, but, on the other hand, if you hem yourself in to your storyboards, you limit your possibilities. You won't ever discover those magical moments that occur on set. The actors are in the environment outlined in the script for the first time and they use their intuition to block the scene. Often, it stifles actors if a director blocks a scene before they've tried it themselves. When you're going for a complicated camera move that demands elaborate choreography, then it makes sense to dictate blocking. Most of the time, it's best to let the actors have the first stab.

The biggest discovery in this film is, without a doubt, Cynda Williams. She's star material, you heard it here first. Considering that this is Cynda's first film, her scene presence is amazing. Her eyes are her best features. She really knows how to use them. She rolls her eyes and flutters her lashes in the most seductive way. Cynda has actually made me more aware of how important the eyes are in acting.

On Tuesday, we shot Bleek and Clarke doing the mo' better and the scene that follows it, Clarke biting Bleek's lip. After seeing the dailies the next evening I decided to do a reshoot. Cynda was supposed to appear naked, but you could see her panties in the shot. Also, on some of the takes she seemed a bit conscious of her exposed breasts.

We filmed our first big makeup scene on Wednesday. Special-effects makeup artist Tom Bromberg created a grotesque scar for Bleek's upper lip for the scene of him bugging out after the accident. He lies on the floor of the loft caught in a painful hallucination. Though it's a simple scene, Denzel's performance is very effective.

The following day we shot what I feel is my best acting to date, the scene where Bleek fires me as his manager. We did a close-up of Giant telling Bleek that his gambling is a sickness. It came to me to have the camera spin on its axis as a way of expressing visually what's happening to Giant. It cuts nicely with the shot that follows of Giant asleep on Bleek's couch. With unconventionally angled shots, there's always the danger of making your audience too aware of the camera. I don't mind the risk. I didn't want this film to look like your average Hollywood fare: master shot, medium shot, close-up, close-up. I hate this type of filmmaking.

With this film I've been my most assertive as far as blocking shots for the camera. Ernest has an excellent visual sense, and in the past I might have leaned on him a little bit too much. Ernest and I were still collaborating 100 percent on *Mo' Better Blues*, but I did my best to take the initiative more.

Friday night we cruised through the scene of Clarke trying to talk Bleek into letting her sing with the band and Clarke trying, once again, to seduce Bleek while he's playing the piano. We wrapped early because Denzel wanted to go to L.A. to spend the weekend with his family.

Our fourth week went by quickly. The week's dailies looked good. Jim Jacks, one of the executives at Universal, came by the set on Friday. Saturday morning my editor, Sam Pollard, and I showed Jim selected dailies at our cutting room at Forty Acres and a Mule Filmworks.

I've been worrying lately that something is wrong with my memory. There are so many things that happen to me in a given week that I can't recall—so much information that anything that is not of upmost importance, I forget. If I didn't, I would be bogged down with useless data. Often, I ask friends if they've seen a certain movie, and they remind me that it was I who took them to see it. I got a lot on my mind. Only the most important stuff sticks. It's sad, but I guess that's the way it is.

WEEK FIVE: OCTOBER 23-27, 1989

On Tuesday and Wednesday, we shot one of the most difficult scenes of the film: Bleek makes love to Clarke and Indigo at the same time. Love scenes can be difficult if actors don't feel comfortable. Denzel Washington is a great actor and a sex symbol, but he's very uncomfortable with sex scenes. He refused to take off his shirt in this scene. Both Indigo and Clarke are topless but he said, "I'm not taking my shirt off. I already did one love scene without my shirt." He said, "I've made love with my T-shirt on plenty of times."

There's a shot where we're on Cynda's hands as they travel down Denzel's back and right where we get to his butt we stop panning and go back up. My first assistant picture editor, Brunilda Torres, asked, "Why don't we get to see his butt?" I wasn't averse to it, but Denzel said from the very beginning, "I ain't no William Hurt. I'm not showing my butt in this film."

When I do another film that involves love scenes, I'll use a male star who is not averse to nudity. If I play a role and we have to see my butt when I'm getting out of bed or something, it's okay. I find it unfair that you always see a woman's body parts on film but seldom a man's. I know many women out there who wanted to see Denzel's butt. But he wasn't going for it.

I don't think Denzel ever moves his pelvis or his butt in any of the film's love scenes. He would often say to me, "Spike, I got two sons. I can't be doing this kind of stuff." Of course, he never told me that before we started to shoot the film. Regardless, the man is still a great actor and I'm glad the Academy thinks so also.

Thursday and Friday we shot the dinner party. It was a hard two days for me because we used smoke to enhance the ambience of the scene and it made me sick. Usually smoke doesn't bother me. The prop department must have used a different type because I was wheezing, sick as a dog both days. Those were the last two days of the ten that we shot at Bleek's loft.

It was a night shoot. We used red and blue gels on the lights. I told Ernest I wanted the set to be dark like a house party. Also, the less light we had inside, the more we could see the view outside the windows—the Brooklyn Bridge, the Manhattan skyline.

We had almost all the principal actors on set. Joe Seneca came in to play Big Stop's friend. Branford Marsalis came in to play himself. We did a lot of ad-libbing. Linda Hawkins, who plays Jeanne, Left Hand Lacey's French girlfriend, has a cameo in the party scene. Linda and I met at the American pavilion at the 1989 Cannes Film Festival. American students who speak French are employed there. When it came time to cast the film, I remembered to give Linda an audition. I had a hard time finding a White actress who fit the character. Linda, to be frank, wasn't that good, but I got the idea to do the character as a Frenchwoman. Left Hand could have met her in Paris or France somewhere and asked her to come back to the States with him. So Linda auditioned as a Frenchwoman and gave a much better performance. That's how she got the role.

The party scene begins with Big Stop and Joe Seneca's character cooking gumbo. Everything we ate and drank in the scene was real—even the beer.

We wrapped early Saturday morning and I drove down to D.C. to Howard University's homecoming, wheezing all the way. Really, I was wheezing the entire weekend.

On Monday we went back to the location of day one to shoot our final scene. The four kids who began the film came back to play friends of young Miles. We had three setups to do that day and we ran late. It got too dark to do our final shot, which was a drag because it had been a beautiful day. We had to come back early Tuesday morning to do the shot, even though there was a threat of rain.

The Louma crane captured the kids running down the block. They run past the camera, then we tilt down to a little girl drawing "The End" in the street. The idea for the shot came from the *Do the Right Thing* poster.

We had to deal with the problem that this scene takes place ten years in the future. Rather than worry about getting hold of futuristic prop cars, I decided not to use cars at all. We rented playground equipment and made the street into a playground. We took thirty-five kid extras, put them in a lot of bright ski clothing, and had them play in the street. That's how we got around not having the budget to fill the block with cars of the future.

We finished the rest of the montage shots on Tuesday. The entire day was spent in Big Stop's house. I added a shot of Indigo going in labor. I think that we did it very nonstereotypically. In most films you see the husband getting hysterical when his wife goes into labor. Denzel and Joie played it calmly.

Wednesday was great. We were at Harlem Hospital filming the birth of Miles Gilliam. In preproduction we were faced with the question: Should we do this live? I always thought we should. The real problem was finding a hospital to accommodate us, and Harlem Hospital did. We selected a date, November 1. The hospital put us in touch with women who were having babies around that date. We got a few to sign releases saying that we could film them giving birth, in exchange for a fee.

The morning we arrived, one of the women was in labor. She had a hard labor and took a long time, so we had enough time to film another shot, which was Bleek and Indigo driving up to the hospital in a cab. That was probably the hardest shot that day 'cause you're talking about 135th Street and Lenox Avenue. There's a subway stop right there and we attracted a big crowd. It was morning rush hour. It was hard to get people not to look into the camera.

We filmed two births that day. Both babies were delivered by Dr. Sterling Williams, who is the hospital's director of obstetrics and gynecology. As soon as we finished filming the first woman, the other was ready to have her baby. We had to squash lunch and run to the other delivery room. That baby came out fast.

MO'
BETTER
NOTES

I had a good talk with the woman's husband. Two weeks before, she told him, "Spike Lee wants to put me in his movie having a kid." He said, "Honey, you're crazy. Even if that's true, how do you know you're going to have the kid on November first?" "I'll have it November first if it kills me!" she said. His wife wasn't in labor when they came to the hospital, but when she heard we were filming the first woman, she went into labor. Ironically, both children were girls, but you really won't be able to tell on the screen.

It's gonna be a great sequence. There's never been a scene in a film of a Black woman giving birth. Yeah, there was "Roots," but you don't see no kid popping out a vagina.

I was in the delivery room, but I didn't watch either birth in its entirety because there wasn't enough room for me to get a clear view. I did manage to see one kid come out. It's just amazing, the whole reproduction thing.

The crew was overwhelmed. Jonathan Burkhardt, the first assistant camera operator, and Nike Zachmanoglou, the continuity person, both came up to me afterward to say thank you—Nike even gave me a kiss. I felt like I was the father.

We came back to Harlem on Thursday and Friday to shoot Indigo waiting on her stoop for Bleek. He arrives, brings her to the apartment, and they make love. Our location for this scene is a wonderful brownstone on 141st Street between Convent Avenue and Hamilton Place. The residents were very gracious. We also shot Bleek ringing Indigo's doorbell after bombing out at the "Dizzy Club." To create the effect of rain in that shot we used rain towers. Rain towers are really just a large sprinkler system that allows water to cascade down from high above a set.

WEEK SEVEN: NOVEMBER 6-10, 1989

Monday and Tuesday we were at the America restaurant on East 18th Street in Manhattan, our location for the "Dizzy Club." We had a big exterior scene to shoot on Monday. We only had two setups, a Louma crane shot and a Steadicam shot, but they were very involved. We used rain towers again and lots of extras.

The first shot follows Bleek after he has bombed out onstage. He comes out of the club and gives his trumpet to Giant, now the doorman at the "Dizzy." I follow Bleek down the block yelling at him. We did eight or nine takes of that. The first take was the only one in focus. Thank God there was one!

For the Steadicam shot we used Ted Churchill, the top Steadicam man in New York. We wanted it to be a fluid shot. It begins on a wall plastered with photos of the Shadow Henderson Quartet (we planned to superimpose "One Year Later" here). Denzel steps into the frame of the camera and looks toward us. The camera moves around Denzel, over his shoulder. We now see what he's looking at: the "Dizzy Club." We follow Denzel across the street and end up in a two-shot of Bleek and Giant. They haven't seen each other in a year and they go on inside the club together

On Tuesday we shot "Harlem Blues" and Bleek bombing out onstage. You should see the look on Denzel's face when he crumbles. It's a killer. We had a club full of three hundred extras, our regular crew, and additional crew members. It was madness. We didn't get out until eight in the morning. We should have had two days to shoot "Harlem Blues" instead of one, but we couldn't afford it. Buying out the restaurant for two days (one for the exterior of the "Dizzy" and one for "Harlem Blues") cost us a ton.

Most of the extras in the club are Black even though we comment in the script about the fact that Whites tend to patronize jazz clubs more than Blacks. I wanted to give Black actors jobs. Anyway, you won't be able to tell if the extras are Black or White because they're in the background for the most part. In many ways this film is a romantic ideal of the jazz world. It's my version of this particular story.

For the next three days we were in "Shinbone Alley," off Bond Street, between Broadway and Lafayette. Wednesday was a very light day because we were burnt out from the previous two days. Thursday and Friday we shot the scenes of Giant and Bleek getting beaten up by the hoods. It's a make-or-break scene. We did twenty-four setups Friday. We rocked the house.

Jeff Ward, the stunt coordinator, looked through the camera on every shot. If the storyboard called for a right, but because of where the camera was placed a right looked fake and a left looked better, we changed the punch to a left.

Our bloody faces were courtesy of Tom Bromberg. Tom is a top special-effects makeup man in NABET, the union we've used on this film. He wrote me a nice letter commenting on how much he liked the script. Tom was also responsible for Bleek's fucked-up lip in its various stages of healing. Tom gave me a heavy-duty makeup job for the fight scene. I had pads in my mouth for swelling. My left eye was covered completely. Being one-eyed like that really messes with your equilibrium. Between takes I put my glasses on over the one good eye.

The ass-kicking that Giant receives is brutal, but also very funny. Rod and Madlock use his head as a football and kick a field goal. These guys are not your stereotypical goons. They're sadists, but funny sadists. These guys just enjoy inflicting pain. They love it—it's not just a job.

Over the weekend we pulled selected takes for Universal. They didn't bug us to see dailies every single day like studios often do other filmmakers. They were so good about leaving me alone that I sent them two hours' worth of stuff.

WEEK EIGHT: NOVEMBER 13–17, 1989

We didn't shoot the first day of this week. We spent it loading equipment and setting the lights at our soundstage, Empire Stages in Long Island City. Empire is a small stage. It fit our size needs and our budget.

To create "Beneath the Underdog," Wynn Thomas did the research that any good production designer would do. He visited jazz clubs in New York. Most of the clubs are holes in the wall. Our set looks like a ballroom by comparison. I know we'll be accused of romanticizing jazz clubs because there are no clubs, at least in New York, as big or elaborate as the ones in this film. I asked Wynn to connect as many rooms of the set as possible. This would allow us to do traveling shots from room to room.

The weekend before we had a photo shoot for the movie poster. Bill Claxton, a famous jazz photographer, shot it. He's done tons of album covers, many for the Blue Note label. I ran across a book of Claxton's photographs while doing research for the film. It included Claxton's famous photographs of Chet Baker and his two wives. When I saw those shots I wanted to use the same compositions for the movie poster. Universal tracked down Claxton. He's currently an art director for *Motor Trend* magazine in Los Angeles. He was happy to have the opportunity to do this for me. I told him at the end of the shoot that if we were going to steal his ideas, we might as well hire him to do the job.

Throughout the film, we hear Bleek complain about the bad deal Giant cut with Moe and Josh Flatbush, owners of "Beneath the Underdog." The exploitation of the artist is a theme that pops up often in this film. It wasn't very pronounced in the script, but once you start shooting, things that seemed subordinate come out. Ad-libs by John and Nick Turturro, who play the Flatbush brothers, had a lot to do with it. At one point the house comedian, Butterbean Jones, played by the late, great Robin Harris, says, "I want a raise, motherfuckers!"

Everyone remembers John Turturro as Pino in *Do the Right Thing*. We used his younger brother Nick a lot on the dubbing for *Do the Right Thing*. I knew that he and John would have no problem playing brothers. And I think John was elated to have done a movie with his brother, who is a less experienced actor.

This production seemed to go more quickly than any of my others. It was an easier film to shoot than *Do the Right Thing*—or it seemed that way, even though *Mo' Better Blues* required far more locations.

We had a wrap ceremony, as we always do, led by our co producer, Monty Ross. It was very moving. The cast and crew presented Denzel with a gold trumpet and brought tears to his eyes. I got one as well. There was a powerful feeling among us, a sense of family. There we were, a group of young Black people who had forged ahead and made a difference in the vicious world of Hollywood. We didn't ask anybody for anything—we just came in there and made our own place. We have so much love and respect for each other as Black people who continue to grow in our respective fields. This bond between us may have made some White crew members feel like outsiders, but on wrap day everyone's happy, everyone feels part of the team.

Our crew, this time, was better than ever. On *School Daze* we had a nonunion crew and many who were second-stringers. The film was shot in Atlanta, which doesn't have the same quality of talent as Los Angeles and New York. We had a good union crew on *Do the Right Thing*, but we didn't have NABET's A team. Because of our success with the film, we were able to attract top-notch people. They saw *Do the Right Thing* and heard that we treat our crew and cast very well —nobody gives out jackets and T-shirts like we do.

Aside from the ceremony, we had a leisurely day. We shot my barber, Larry Cherry, giving haircuts to the guys in the band. (This scene didn't make the cut. Larry, this had nothing to do with your acting!) We did a shot of Moe and Josh Flatbush playing the bouncers, Born Knowledge and Eggy, in a game of puff basketball in their office.

We knocked off some shots of the empty club to use in a montage after Bleek and Giant have been beaten up. One shot is of Moe and Josh sitting distraught in the middle of the empty club. One by one the lights go out. The last light off is the spotlight on their table. The spotlight goes out and the club is black. The final shot of the day was of the empty dressing room with a lit cigarette hanging off the side of the sink. (Don't look for this shot in the film, folks—it didn't make the cut either.) We saved these shots for the last day because they weren't crucial, but we thought we might need them—sometimes, in the editing room, you wish you had footage of a certain scene that was scripted, but that you never bothered to shoot.

MO'
BETTER
NOTES

I took home parts of the set for my collection, including a large stained-glass hanging with the "Beneath the Underdog" logo. I have collected too much movie shit over the years. It's getting ridiculous—I have to start letting some of it go. I gotta give some of my clothes away. I have five million T-shirts, mostly presents from folks—I can't wear all that stuff.

A melancholy feeling sets in the day after you wrap a film. On a shoot, you fall into a routine of getting up at 5:30 A.M. every day. When it's over, you kinda miss the torture. It's back to the office to edit and work on the next script.

Not to negate love and relationships, but I don't think *Mo' Better Blues* is as important a film as *Do the Right Thing*. This doesn't mean that I like it less—it was the right film for me to do at the time. However, the issue of racism is one I want to explore again on film.

P O S T P R O D U C T I O N

We began editing *Mo' Better Blues* on December 11, 1989, and completed the rough cut on February 26, 1990. It clocked in at two hours and thirty-one minutes. Long! Too long!! Actually, the first time we counted we miscalculated and added an extra twelve minutes to the film. Twelve minutes is a long time on the big screen.

It took ten weeks for us to arrive at a rough cut. For *Do the Right Thing*, it took only six weeks. The reason for the difference: We printed 125,000 feet of film for *Do the Right Thing*. On *Mo' Better Blues* we shot and printed 300,000 feet. The more film you shoot, the more time you spend viewing and selecting takes. Why did we shoot that much film? Good question. *Mo' Better Blues* had a ten-week shooting schedule, as opposed to the eight weeks we had on *Do the Right Thing*. More importantly, there were seven musical numbers to film, and, in most cases, three cameras rolling on each take. Plenty of film is eaten up right there.

How do you deal with so much footage? Another good question. We work on a Steenbeck editing machine that has two screens. This allows us to look at two reels of footage simultaneously. While my editor and I screen the footage, I comment on the shots and the assistant editors take notes. If it's a musical number, for instance, I might say, "I want to emphasize this segment of the song with a close-up" or "I like the way the camera moves in here." Eventually we select a shot to use as a master, and around it we weave the other shots we've selected for the scene.

I knew all along we'd be faced with a long rough cut of *Mo' Better Blues*. Every day of the editing process I asked myself, "Which scenes can we trim? Which scenes can we lose?" I was sad to part with "M & N," but watching the film now, I can't say I miss it. Some scenes that don't work for the film leap out at you right away, others take you a while to discover. One of the reasons I find research screenings helpful is I can use the audiences to clue me in to what works and what doesn't. I don't have to read the response cards to know the deal. Sitting in the back of the movie theater and listening to the audience's response, or lack thereof, is enough for me.

For *Mo' Better Blues* we held two research screenings, one in Chicago and one in Philadelphia. The big cheeses at Universal saw the film for the first time on March 27, 1990, the day after the Academy Awards. They were pleased overall, but they felt that the film was still too long.

Because we moved the release date from fall to summer 1990, we had less time to cut this film than we had to cut *Do the Right Thing*. To make our deadline for a rough cut, the editors had to work seven days a week. *Mo' Better Blues* marked the first time that I didn't spend every day of the editing process in the cutting room. Since *Do the Right Thing*, my time has been in much demand. I was taken away often on speaking engagements and involved in directing commercials and music videos. Supervising the recording and mixing of the soundtrack was another time-consuming task.

I edited *She's Gotta Have It* myself. Barry Alexander Brown edited *School Daze* and *Do the Right Thing*. Barry had the chance to write and direct his first feature, *Lonely in America*, at the same time we were going into production on *Mo' Better Blues*. I was forced to look for a new editor. Eventually I decided on a veteran editor named Sam Pollard. Sam has done most of his work in documentaries— this is his first full-length feature. What sold me on Sam is his love and knowledge of jazz. Before starting *Mo' Better Blues*, he cut a documentary on Max Roach. It was a pleasure working with Sam. I won't go into comparisons between him and Barry. Both have done a fine job making sense of my footage.

From the opening credit sequence.

The full-cast read-through of the script (*from left*): Robin Harris, Denzel Washington, Bill Nunn.

▼

First day of shooting: Watching on the video monitors as the Louma crane goes through the opening shot of
the film.

▼

Brooklyn, New York, 1969: Bleek, come on out ya fuckin' bum.

Working with kids is murder!

▼

Zakee Howze as the young Bleek/young Miles.

▼

Giancarlo Esposito and Linda Hawkins meeting for the first time at the full-cast read-

through (*left*), and as Left Hand Lacey and his French girlfriend, Jeanne (*right*).

▼

Big Stop and young Bleek.

▼

Father and son.

▼

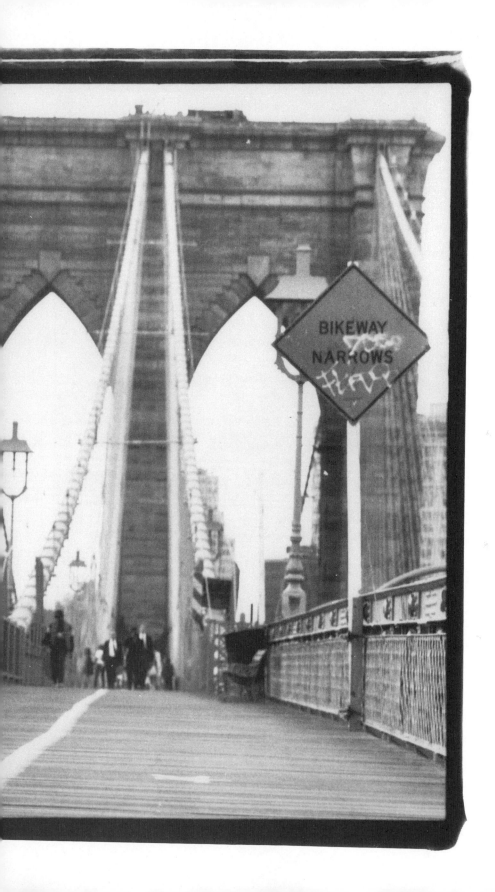

Brooklyn Bridge.

▼

Cynda, Denzel, and Miles coolin' on the set.

▼

▼

Butterbean warms up.

▼

Josh, Bleek, and Moe.

▼

Squabbling over money with the Flatbush brothers.

▼

Giant rides the dolly.

▼

Harlem brownstone.

▼

**MO'
BETTER
BLUES**

The first stunt work I ever did. All praises due, I didn't get injured.

Madlock (Sam Jackson) to Giant: ''We don't believe in killing our brothers and sisters.''

▼

Giant gets the ax.

▼

Madlock (*left*) and Rod (Leonard Thomas) wear out Giant in the alley.

▼

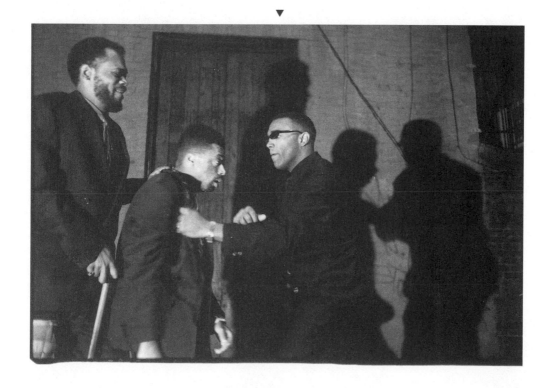

Giant, wake up!

▼

Bleek to the rescue.

▼

Bleek gets housed with his own trumpet.

▼

Just plain fucked up.

▼

Moe Flatbush
demands that the
band go back
onstage.

Can't play anymore.

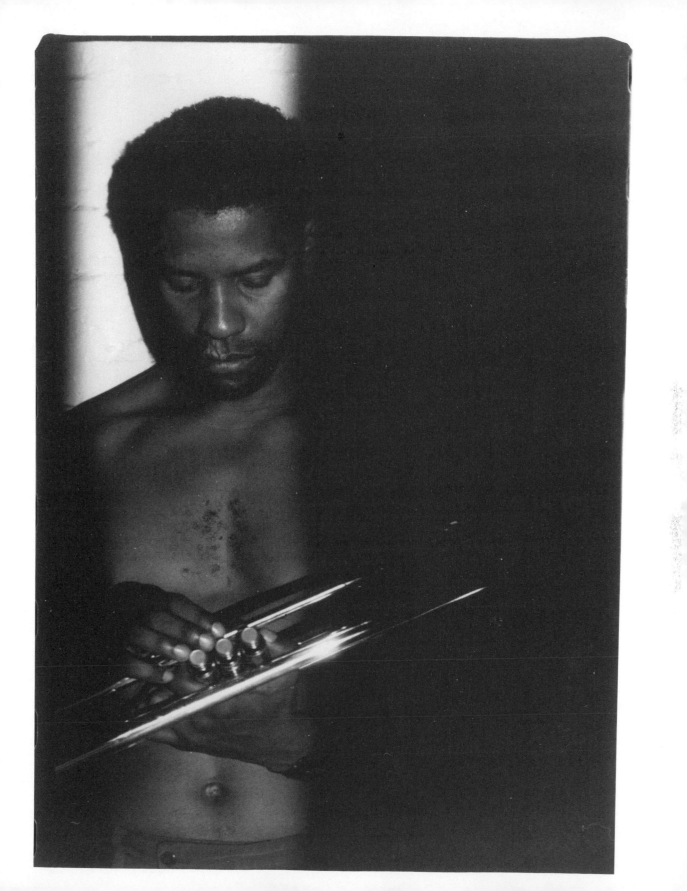

One year later.

▼

Bleek bolts from the "Dizzy Club" after bombing out onstage. That's the Louma crane, *left,* and Giant, *right,* in hot pursuit.

▼

Bleek, I won't sell it. I won't sell it.

▼

Bleek asks Indigo to ''save my life'': the hardest scene to direct.

▼

The kiss.

Bleek's boys wish him well.

▼

Surrounded by in-laws at the wedding.

▼

Feels good.

▼

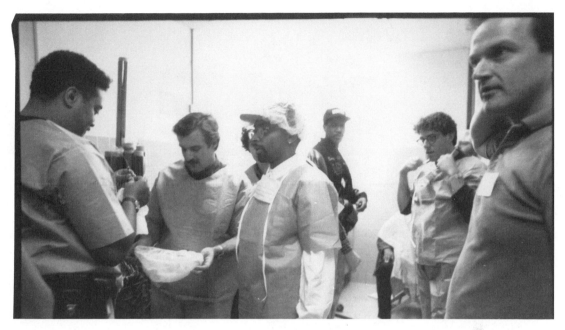

Preparing to film in the delivery room of Harlem Hospital.

▼

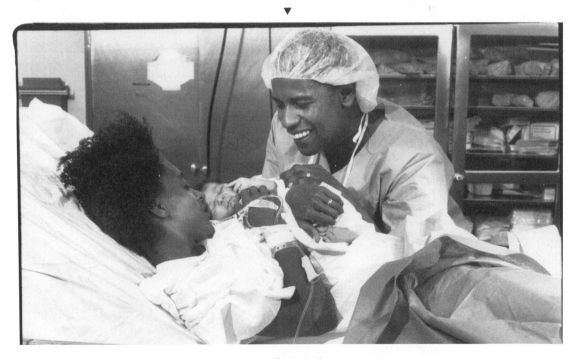

The birth of Miles Gilliam.

▼

Grandfather Big Stop and one of the five children who played young Miles.

▼

From the *Love Supreme* montage.

▼

Father and son.

▼

With Ernest on location for the final shot of the film.

MO'
BETTER
BLUES

The Key Cogs *(left to right)*: Ernest Dickerson, Robi Reed, Monty Ross, Wynn Thomas, and Jon Kilik.

▼

Mo'Better crew (and some cast members), final day of shoot.

▼

Love Supreme to *Variations on the Mo' Better Blues* to *Mo' Better Blues.*

▼

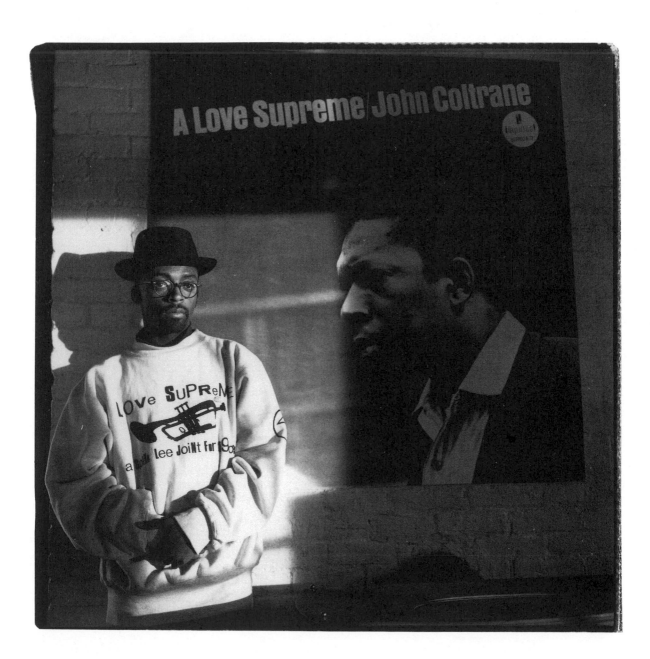

The set of "Beneath the Underdog," where we spent the last three weeks of production. Notice the cityscape in the right corner.

BENEATH THE UNDERDOG
W Y N N   T H O M A S

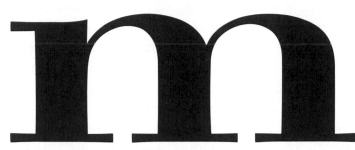y first conversation with Spike about *Mo' Better Blues* took place on January 1, 1989. He called to wish me Happy New Year and talk about what he was calling *Love Supreme* at the time. He was adamant that the film shouldn't look like *Bird*. I told him that nothing should look like *Bird*—it was far too dark. Then again, jazz films have always been shot on dark sets that feel like little black boxes.

I didn't do much research between my initial talk with Spike and my first reading of the script. As a production designer, I find it dangerous to research before reading the script. I might fall in love with an image that doesn't necessarily work with the script and wind up imposing it on the film. Production design should first and foremost be influenced by the script.

My first week on the job was all leg work. Line producer Jon Kilik and I visited jazz clubs in Manhattan. I decided that our club should be less like a traditional jazz hole in the wall and more like a spacious nightclub, so I went to the library and researched nightclubs. I looked at clubs from the '20s and '30s in particular. I was interested in how they treated space, especially the relationship of audience to performers.

Research does two things for me: Either it confirms what I have in my head or it tells me I'm doing something wrong. And what this research did was confirm that there was a time period in which clubs were colorful and bright as opposed to dark and dank. I began calling our jazz club a jazz nightclub to change the way we were conceiving it.

Another characteristic of jazz films of the past is their generally uninteresting camera angles. High-angle shots are rare, and most of the time the camera is static. I decided it was crucial to design a two-story club to give Spike and Ernest the possibility of high-angle shots, and of using the Louma crane (as well as having enough space on set to contain it). The space would allow for a lyrical rather than static use of the camera, an approach more consistent with the spirit and movement of jazz music.

The name of the club, "Beneath the Underdog," was also an important inspiration for the design. It helped me map out the dimensions of the space. I placed the main room in a basement so the audience enters on street level and descends into the club. I knew there would be a stage at one end of the main room, a bar at the other, and a balcony space above. The shape of the club blossomed from there. The backstage and owners' office fell into place later on.

I had a hard time at first justifying the shape of the club. On film it's realistic, but in terms of architectural conventions it's not. You descend into the club, then the main room shoots up practically twenty feet high—a design like that is highly unlikely. It was an unusual choice for me because it was abstract.

I was so concerned about whether this choice would work that I ran it by a fellow designer whom I respect. She told me that a production designer's common impulse is to make everything real. But as a designer matures, he or she begins to look at the abstract as a choice that's often more emotionally realistic or appropriate. Our conversation gave me more confidence about my design choices. I was still making choices that I wasn't entirely sure about, but I believe they worked for the picture.

With my ground plan in hand, I drafted each room of the club individually. If you were to look at my sketch of the club's main room, you'd see the stage and its proscenium. To the left and right of the proscenium are two doors. In that first sketch, I established a style of architecture for the entire club. From there, full-scale drawings were done of every single detail, from the door handles to the cornices. Many of the club's design elements were influenced by Art Deco. One of the reasons I chose Art Deco was that it deals with straight lines. I hoped to keep my cost down by using Art Deco, as opposed to Art Nouveau, which is all curves and swirls and is more expensive to construct.

Spike specifically asked for an image of a foot crushing a dog as a logo for "Beneath the Underdog." I drafted the logo, but continued to ask myself, "Who is the underdog?" For me, New York City became the underdog. Those who live here are beneath the city: It dwarfs us with its tall buildings, asphyxiates us with its pollution, and pushes us to the edge with its pace. This idea gave birth to the "Beneath the Underdog" cityscape, a cyclorama of a city skyline mounted above the club's main room. Lights are projected through windows in the cyclorama, giving the feel of a brightly lit city at night. The audience appears to be sitting beneath the city.

Initially I thought the cityscape would be a problem for Ernest and the gaffer, Charles Houston. It was exciting to find out that it wasn't a problem at all—in fact, they used it as a lighting source. Ernest was also able to change the atmosphere of the club by projecting different colors through the cyclorama. What started as an aesthetic touch on my part turned out to be a functional fixture on set. That's the wonderful thing about the collaboration of Spike, Ernest, and myself: One person contributes an idea, and the next person comes along and embellishes it.

It took me three weeks to show Spike a rough ground plan of the club. (In its final form the set was not significantly different from that plan.) Once Spike approved the ground plan, we booked Empire Stages. We taped out the dimensions of the soundstage floor to give Spike a sense of the set's components.

We began building right after Labor Day. We were supposed to build for eight weeks, but it took us eleven. The frame of the club—the actual walls—went up rather quickly. What took longer than anticipated was the treatment of surfaces (aging of wallpaper, for example) and installation of details, like door fixtures and what we call chair rails, moldings that run around the room.

Spike and I talked about the history of the club. Moe and Josh Flatbush, the current owners, are the sons of the original owners. The club would have been built in the late 1930s. Moe and Josh's office hasn't changed since Moe senior occupied it. This is how I justified the lush, old-world feel of their office.

If the club was built in the late '30s, it would stand to reason that musicians like Duke Ellington and Cab Calloway could have performed there. In fact, as part of my design subtext, I decided that "Beneath the Underdog" had a rich history of jazz, from the big-band era to the contemporary generation of artists represented by Bleek. The next generation, represented by the Shadow Henderson Quintet, goes off to play the "Dizzy Club," a larger, less intimate venue.

Thinking about the production design of *Mo' Better Blues* as a whole, it seems like we made a period film without specifying a period. The interior of the club is from the '30s. The exterior was inspired by West 52nd Street at its peak in the '50s. Bleek's loft has the clutter and character of artists' spaces of the late '60s, not the empty, sterile lofts of the '80s. It's my hope the mixed time periods will give the movie a sense of timelessness.

▼

three

mo'
BETTER
MUSIC

azz has been an integral part of all my movies. My father has scored every film I've done since my second year at film school, and all these scores have been jazz-based. Back in '85, the writer Nelson George, who invested in *She's Gotta Have It*, begged me to reconsider the film's jazz score. He thought that young people into hip-hop wouldn't be able to relate to jazz and the film would suffer at the box office. Certainly jazz has never detracted from the appeal of my films. If anything, it's made them better films. I use jazz because it lends a sense of tradition and timelessness. And a musical score should enhance a film, not just accompany it.

Mo' Better Blues has a jazz score, and the featured music, songs played on screen by the Bleek Quintet, are jazz compositions. Except for a couple of numbers, I wanted the music to be "straight-ahead" classical jazz—acoustic and very melodic. Definitely not fusion, in the vein of Kenny G, or free jazz, like the music of Sun Ra or Ornette Coleman.

I knew that the average moviegoing audience is not the same audience that frequents jazz clubs, and they won't come to a theater to sit through a fifteen-minute musical number. Even though we shot seven musical numbers, I realized that I faced some critical decisions down the line about which songs would be cut down or cut out entirely. It's a shame, because they're all good songs. But the reality is that this film couldn't have been much more than two hours long. If we had included complete songs, it would have been much longer than that. One day I'd like to release a two-and-a-half-hour version with all the musical numbers intact.

Music plays such an important part in my films that, even before I write the script, I have in my mind which musicians and composers will be involved in the project. For *Mo' Better Blues*, I wanted Branford Marsalis' group to record all the featured music, which includes songs written by him and by my father, Bill Lee. Branford's band is Bob Hirsh on bass, Jeff Watts on drums, Kenny Kirkland

MO'
BETTER
MUSIC

on piano, and the man himself on tenor and soprano saxophone. The only problem was that the main character of the film plays trumpet. At Branford's suggestion, I contacted Terence Blanchard, who played with Art Blakey and later headed his own quintet with saxophonist Donald Harrison. So whenever you hear the Bleek Quintet on film, you're really listening to the Branford Marsalis Quartet with Terence Blanchard on trumpet.

I told Branford about the idea for the film quite early on, in hopes of getting him to play Shadow. Branford played one of the Fellas in *School Daze*. He's done a few film roles since, including a role in *Throw Momma from the Train*, with Danny DeVito. I first saw Branford on screen in *Bring on the Night*, a concert film on British rock star Sting and his band of Black musicians. I liked Branford's energy on film, so I asked him to be in *School Daze*.

Branford loved the idea for *Mo' Better Blues* and said he'd play Shadow if his schedule permitted. His schedule didn't allow it after all, but he was able to stay involved with the project by recording the featured music and writing four songs: "Say Hey," the first musical number of the film; "Pop Top 40 R n' B Urban Contemporary Easy Listening Love," which I wrote the lyrics for; and "Knocked out the Box," which the Bleek Quintet plays onstage at "Beneath the Underdog" while Giant is getting beat up in the alley. After we finished shooting, he recorded one more song, called "Beneath the Underdog."

During preproduction, in July '89, Robi Reed and I went to Chicago to do a casting call for the role of Clarke. That same weekend, Branford was booked at a local jazz club. Robi and I dropped by for a set. I gave Branford the lyrics to "Pop Top 40" and went over the instrumental numbers, so he could compose everything in time for our August recording dates at RCA Studios.

It was in Chicago that Branford told me to cast his drummer, Jeff Watts, as Rhythm Jones. He knew the difficulty I was having finding an actor who could drum or a drummer who could act, so he very unselfishly offered Jeff. He canceled an entire month of gigs because he didn't want to play without Jeff. I'm sure Branford lost a bit of money, and I'm grateful to him for the sacrifice.

At the same time, Branford pointed out that it would be nearly impossible for one drummer, let alone an actor with no music training, to "drum-sync" to another drummer's track. Every drummer has his own style, which is hard for another to mimic convincingly. Jeff was our best bet, because he alone could reproduce for camera what he'd do at the recording sessions in August.

The sessions were casual and fast-moving, perhaps because we were working with a quintet rather than the eighty-plus musicians we used on the scores of

School Daze and *Do the Right Thing*. My father and Delfeayo Marsalis, Branford's younger brother who produces his albums, produced all the songs, except for "Harlem Blues," which was done by Raymond Jones. We recorded "Harlem Blues" and the music track of "Pop Top 40" the same night. The remaining numbers took three days

We needed music for the rehearsal scene of "Pop Top 40," so we recorded the song as if the band were playing it for the first time. The musicians had a chance to mess up on purpose, which they enjoyed immensely. Denzel called the studio that night from California. I put the phone next to the speaker and Denzel stayed on the line for a long time listening to Terence play.

Denzel couldn't make it to New York for the initial recording of "Pop Top 40." The music is cued by the vocals, so we couldn't record without a vocal track. Luckily Wesley is based in New York, and he came down to the studio to help us out. Wesley does a few lyrics in the final version, but we had him do a dummy track of the entire song, which we used to lay down the music. When Denzel came into town for rehearsals, we went back into the studio to overdub his vocal track.

"Pop Top 40" was a first for Denzel—he had never recorded a song before. It was hard for him to get the rhythm of the lyrics at first, but he did a fine job in the end. There's a line from "What the World Needs Now" that I worked into "Pop Top 40," and Denzel couldn't sing it on key for the life of him. A dozen takes later, he got it right.

My father gave me many songs to consider for *Mo' Better Blues*. More than half I had to pass on. They were all good pieces of music, but they weren't right, either for the scene in question or for the movie as a whole. When my father played me "Mo' Better Blues," which he originally named "Deep Valley," it struck me as the perfect piece of music to use as Bleek's theme. It's the song Bleek plays at the club after he breaks up with Indigo and Clarke, and it runs over the opening credits. I wrote the piece into the script first as "Both My Women Done Left Me Blues," but later changed the title to reflect the new name of the film.

My father wrote the song that Bleek plays, or tries to play, one year after his accident, when he sits in at the "Dizzy Club" with his old band, now the Shadow Henderson Quintet. The song was untitled when we recorded it, and for some reason we didn't get around to naming it until late in postproduction. We settled on a simple title: "Again Never." What I like most about this song is that it plays for the length of the scene, after Bleek exits the club, gives his trumpet to Giant, now the "Dizzy Club" doorman, and heads out into the rainy night. Vicious.

A third number my father wrote for the film is "M & N," a children's alphabet song that we recorded with Joie and a chorus of twenty-four kids from the Brooklyn Catholic school where we shot the scene. Despite protests from my father, the scene and the song were subsequently cut from the film. Hey, the rough cut was over two and a half hours long. Something had to go!

While we were taking a break at the studio one night, I overheard Terence tinkering with a melody on the piano. I liked what I heard and asked him to play the entire song. "Sing Soweto" is the title, and Terence agreed to let us use it in the film. That same night, we recorded Terence playing the song as a solo for muted trumpet. It's "Sing Soweto" you hear Bleek play at night on the Brooklyn Bridge. In fact, anytime you hear Bleek playing scales or little riffs on the trumpet, it's Terence. We recorded two hours' worth of this stuff. Terence and I later edited it down to fifteen minutes of material to add to Bleek's repertoire. More work for Denzel!

Next to my father, Terence had the most impact upon how we captured the music on screen. And because of his involvement, I'm sure we've done it, to the best of our abilities, with utmost integrity. Terence made it his personal crusade to see that Denzel looked real on screen—his trumpet techniques, mannerisms, attitude. He wanted Denzel to come across nothing short of a real-life musician.

Any day that Denzel was shooting a scene with music, Terence, as his tutor, was on set lending technical and moral support. And any evening we screened dailies from one of Denzel's music scenes, Terence would be sitting right next to me, hipping me to what was good and bad. It was hundred-percent dedication. That's Terence's personality, though: If he commits to something, he gives it all his energy.

One reason Terence was able to take three months out of his busy life to tutor Denzel was that he was taking a hiatus from performing. Terence was in the process of changing his embouchure, the position and use of his lips in producing notes on the trumpet. Apparently the way he had been taught as a child was incorrect, and he could never get better as a musician unless he changed it. Things worked out well for Terence in the summer of '89: He was able to pick up some extra cash tutoring Denzel, while taking a brief respite from the stage and honing his technique.

After the featured music was recorded in August, we matched each member of the Bleek Quintet, except for Jeff, with a personal music coach. We knew Terence would tutor Denzel as early as June. Bill was assigned to bassist Michael Fleming, an original member of my father's New York Bass Violin Choir, who has recorded and played with many greats, including Coleman Hawkins, Chet Baker, and Rahsaan Roland Kirk. Wesley had trumpeter Donald Harrison, who played with Art Blakey along with Terence, and co-led the Blanchard/Harrison Quintet until they disbanded in '89. Giancarlo had my father and Branford, even though Branford was on the road most of the time. My father started out with Bill, but they didn't hit it off well. We also had problems finding the right coach for Giancarlo, who went through three of them.

The band members and tutors received a cassette tape of each song. On these tapes, each actor had his instrumental part mixed higher than the others. So, if you were the bass player, in your right ear you'd hear your part loud and clear, and in your left ear you'd hear the rest of the ensemble, at a lower volume.

Once I matched the actors with the coaches and saw that everyone had tapes, I let them work out the details of the study process themselves. They met five days a week and each coach had his own approach. Michael Fleming actually taught Bill to play the bass—notes, chords, and everything. Terence concentrated on teaching Denzel the fingering to each tune and how to "sing" the melodies, so that even if he pressed a wrong valve, he'd still be believable and in time with the music. I had confidence in each coach's method, and I didn't interfere. Besides, with preproduction well under way, I had too much other shit to do.

The Bleek Quintet got together with their instruments for the first time during the two-week rehearsal period in September. They still couldn't play well together, even along with the track. It was just a bunch of noise, and nothing was accomplished. We decided that it was better if they continued to practice alone with their coaches.

Bill started learning the bass in June. He was still in Atlanta at the time, but he picked one out and I sent him six hundred dollars to buy it. He didn't start working with Michael Fleming until he got to New York in August. Mike called me one time to say that Bill had missed three lessons in a row. Bill was hiding from him. I found out later that Bill had been practicing so hard his hands were bleeding. He needed the break.

Interestingly enough, it was Giancarlo, who had studied the piano before, who turned out to be the problem student. Giancarlo (or "G-Money," a nickname he picked up on *School Daze*) already had a piano in his house. He was dead set on learning the exact same notes that Kenny Kirkland plays on the track. Kenny is a very accomplished pianist with an inimitable style. I warned Giancarlo that copying him would prove to be impossible.

Near the end of the shoot, Giancarlo finally agreed to do what I told him to do from the start: place his hands in the vicinity of the keys and move in time with his part. Even though Giancarlo was the only one who knew how to play an instrument before we started, his playing is not the most believable on screen. We cut around Giancarlo's piano work more than any other actor's musical performance. This does not detract from his performance overall, which I was very pleased with, especially in the dressing room scene, where his character, Left Hand Lacey, defends his White girlfriend.

Though the crash courses were taxing, I think the actors in the band got into the music. Except for Jeff, once again, it was the first time they had listened to this much jazz—not just tunes composed for the film, but other music recommended by their coaches. They each took the time to check out the music live, especially Bill, who started hanging out with his coach at jazz clubs in the city.

It made sense for us to save all the music scenes for late in our shooting schedule to give the actors as much time as possible to practice. They'd meet the day before filming each musical number to practice as a group for a final time. I couldn't be present at these meetings because I was shooting. Perhaps it was apropos that the Bleek Quintet's first music scene was the rehearsal of "Pop Top 40." Following that, we shot "Harlem Blues," at the "Dizzy Club."

"Harlem Blues" is my favorite number. Raymond Jones, who has written and produced songs for my film soundtracks since *School Daze*, first played me the tune when we were in the studio for *Do the Right Thing*. It was written in the 1920s by composer W. C. Handy ("Father of the Blues"); Raymond put a new melody to the song, but kept the original lyrics, which include some Harlem slang expressions of the day. Raymond did have to switch around the pronouns because the song was written for a male singer.

You'll notice that "Harlem Blues" is not scripted. I never made a formal revision to the script, but it was added after I decided that Clarke should be a good singer and not just a wannabee. Raymond's arrangement of "Harlem Blues" had been in the back of my mind for a year. Not only is it a great song, but it was the perfect vehicle for Cynda Williams' debut as a singer.

Before we moved to the "Beneath the Underdog" set to shoot the bulk of the music scenes, we spent a day rehearsing. We ran the prerecorded music track (called "playback" in film jargon) and walked through each song. There were plenty of wrinkles to iron out, and the musicians were sent home to do their homework. The hardest tune to film was "Pop Top 40," because Denzel and Wesley had to lip-sync rap lyrics and keep up with the music track. The actors came up with their own choreography, which was another thing to factor into the equation.

Every time we shot with playback, the music coaches were on set. They sat around the video monitors watching their pupils. After each take, they would scurry onstage for private conferences with their pupils. When the necessary adjustments or corrections were made, we'd go for another take. The coaches seemed pleased with the actors' performances. There were some things that Denzel did at first that I didn't feel were appropriate. He seemed too flamboyant, holding the trumpet with one hand like a fusion all-star, and not like a jazz traditionalist. Before I had a chance to mention it to Denzel, Terence was on the case. Anyway, it was best that Terence talk to him about trumpet technique. Terence had the expertise and Denzel respected his opinion.

The most difficult overall sequence involving music was Branford's tune "Knocked out the Box," which plays while Giant gets his ass kicked in the alley. We covered the scene extensively, doing many setups. It was necessary because a lot happens: Giant is dragged out of the club and Denzel has a tricky solo, after which he leaves the stage, followed by the band.

When we shoot a musical number, first we film action that covers the entire length of the song, then we take close-ups that emphasize a particular lyric or instrumental accent. Shooting scenes to playback is something I'm very familiar with, having done it since *She's Gotta Have It*. In *School Daze*, our main playback number was "Straight and Nappy," the dance duel between the Wannabees and Jigaboos over "good" and "bad" hair. Most music videos are shot to playback, and I've done my share of these.

In *Mo' Better Blues* we were lucky to have three cameras on set for most of our music scenes. This enabled us to triple our coverage without adding the extra time. Of course, this made things complex for Ernest. He had to light the set to accommodate each camera and make sure they weren't visible to each other.

One of the things I love most about filmmaking is gathering together talented people. To me, Black people are the most creative people on this earth. I'm thankful that my position as an artist has allowed me to work with a few of the giants. I can say, let's call Stevie Wonder, or let's use Al Jarreau for this, or have Branford Marsalis perform that. Let's cast Ossie Davis and Ruby Dee. Or let's call up Coretta Scott King and ask her for permission to use a quote from Martin Luther King, or let's talk to Betty Shabazz. I can go directly to these people and tap into a wealth of Black talent.

One expression of this in *Mo' Better Blues* is the collection of classics that I was given permission to use as incidental music. (This includes all the music that was not part of my father's score or played on screen by the Bleek Quintet.) The most prominent piece of music is Part I of John Coltrane's *A Love Supreme*, the "Acknowledgement" section, but there are others: "Footprints" by Wayne Shorter, "All Blues" by Miles Davis, and "Mercy, Mercy, Mercy" by Cannonball Adderley. Though we paid for the right to use these songs, I'm sure money wasn't the only factor in the decision to grant us permission. Trust in the quality of my work was a strong consideration.

Mo' Better Blues gave me the perfect excuse to add to my jazz library. It's not as big as it should be, but I'm getting there. I often think that if my father weren't a jazz musician, I would never have been exposed to the music. I wouldn't have heard it on the radio, that's for sure. If you don't hear stuff, you'll never develop a taste for it. So much good jazz music just goes unheard.

I'm curious as to how the jazz aficionados will react to the film. Will they judge it solely as a panacea for films like *Bird* and *Round Midnight*, or will they see it as a separate entity? I didn't make this film out of some lofty mission to bring jazz to the masses. If people are exposed to jazz through this film, that's wonderful. I hope that *A Love Supreme* sells two hundred thousand more copies because of *Mo' Better Blues*, but ultimately that's not the reason I made this film. This was simply the film I had in me at the time.

D A D D Y

When I was little I always found it amusing that my father, a small man, played such a big instrument, the bass. My earliest recollection of my father is of him lugging that bass around. Other kids, my friends in particular, had fathers with regular nine-to-five jobs, but I had a musician for a father, and it's been a great influence.

I always looked forward to the Newport Jazz Festival. Daddy would pack all four of us in the Citroën station wagon and drive to Rhode Island, where he accompanied artists like Odetta, Judy Collins, Peter, Paul and Mary, and Josh White. I would tell everyone, "That's my father up there onstage, Bill Lee, he plays bass." Being the firstborn, I probably rebelled against being a musician, although I did choose to take piano, violin, and guitar lessons at various points in my childhood.

Jazz was the first music I ever heard, along with the blues, spirituals, and folk music. As I grew older and developed my own musical tastes, I wanted to listen to Motown and, yes, even to the Beatles, but my father wasn't having it. He didn't want that "bad music" played in our house, so I had to listen to it at a very low volume or just wait till he wasn't around.

In the mid-'60s, the Fender bass became the instrument of the moment. My father refused to play this electric bass. In fact, he refused, and still refuses, to play any form of electric music. He believes in, and will die for, acoustic music— "tone as is," he calls it. Also around this time, my father put an end to his days as an accompanist. He felt the pay wasn't what he deserved and he wanted to do his own shit, so he stopped playing for other people. My mother, Jacquelyn Shelton Lee, went back to work, teaching at St. Ann's, a private school in Brooklyn Heights, so my father could pursue his art. She supported our family until she died of cancer in 1976.

When Daddy did perform, with the Descendants of Mike & Phoebe (a family ensemble) or the New York Bass Violin Choir, I would rarely go. The music was great, but it just killed me that the concerts were so poorly attended. All this great music and the joint would be empty. Those who did come were, for the most part, the friends and relatives of the musicians.

▼

My father had a concert the night the Knicks won their first NBA championship. This was May 8, 1970, the seventh and final game versus the Los Angeles Lakers, and I had a ticket. I went to the game—I had to. My mother was angry as hell. And even though Daddy played it like he didn't care, I know he did.

Now I'm thirty-three years old, making films scored by my father, and more people are hearing his music than ever before. He's finally getting some of the recognition he deserves. He was robbed of an Academy Award nomination for his score of *Do the Right Thing*, his best to date, but I guess you gotta be John Williams to get juice from the Academy.

Bill Lee *(center)* and the New York Bass Violin Choir: On bass *(left to right)*, Lyle Atkinson, Milt Hinton, Richard Davis, Michael Fleming, and Ron Carter; on drums, Al Harewood.

E I G H T
B A R S   I N

B I L L   L E E

Mo' Better Blues will be the fourth feature film score I've done for my son Spike Lee. Right now—as of January 22, 1989, that is—I'm eight bars in. Whether I end up writing more than five hundred sixty bars of music or less, the first eight bars are the most important. My grandfather once told me that if you want to do a job, first get started. Then stick to it everlastingly and, finally, finish it.

My grandfather was the most influential person in my life. He affected the lives of many, but I feel a special connection because I carry his name—William James Edwards. He was born in Snow Hill, Alabama, in a state of poverty, and on top of that he was crippled by a bone disease. It never hindered him from achieving the things that he did.

My grandfather—or Papa, as we called him—went to Tuskegee Institute and became a student of the founder, Booker T. Washington, and of his philosophies. The teaching Papa held most dear was to cast down your buckets where you are. That meant, go back home and uplift the people out of the muck and mire. And that's just what Papa did. He went back home and, in 1893, founded the Snow Hill Institute, a Normal and Industrial School for Colored Boys and Girls, modeled on Tuskegee. This was the time of the great debate between Booker T. Washington and another prominent educator and writer, W. E. B. Du Bois, about whether a Black man should receive an industrial education or a liberal arts education. My grandfather didn't see the division, and the curriculum at Snow Hill reflected this.

Papa was a great orator. He would stir you, that's for sure. He also wrote a book called *Twenty-five Years in the Black Belt*, about his life and work at Snow Hill

Institute. In fact, my grandfather was responsible, in a small way, for seeing that the great American music called bebop came to be.

My grandfather had a smart student named McDuffy who graduated from Snow Hill Institute. He recommended McDuffy to set up a school in Laurinburg, North Carolina, a poor rural area where Black people were just beginning to uplift themselves from slavery. McDuffy founded the Laurinburg Normal and Industrial Institute on the same principles set out by Tuskegee and Snow Hill. Dizzy Gillespie came to study at Laurinburg from Cheraw, South Carolina, which was his home. Of course Dizzy, along with Charlie Parker, gave us bebop, and turned out to be one of the greatest trumpet players in the world. So, that's how my grandfather, through McDuffy, is somehow responsible for the music we call bebop.

My family have always been among the leaders and teachers in Snow Hill, Alabama. Even before Papa built the Institute, my foreparents founded St. Paul A. M. E. Church, which my brothers and sisters and I were made to attend from a young age. I remember the preaching, singing, praying, and shouting done by country preachers who passed through. I loved to hear people harmonize in our church. One woman who sang in the choir had a strange and beautiful way with a harmony. The scale went from one to eight, and this woman would hang on the sixth note, rock back and forth a bit, before going back to the fifth note, the resolution. Her name was Lula Bonner. There were others like her, great singers from the church whom we identified by their way with a song.

Given my family's gift for music, no doubt they were among the anonymous writers of the spirituals. Many folks don't know that the spirituals and work songs were used by the runners of the Underground Railroad. These songs told those who were running how to find the safe spots along the way to freedom. It fascinates me to this day that these freedom songs were sung right in front of slave owners, who understood nothing.

My mother, Alberta G. Lee, was trained at Snow Hill Institute, Fisk University, and the Boston Conservatory of Music as a concert pianist, but she loved popular music. She could pick out pop tunes on the piano by ear. She bought jazz records, especially Louis Armstrong records. When the radio came along, we heard the big bands of the 1930s. Our family had the first radio in Snow Hill—the students at the school gave it to my grandfather for Founder's Day. We would have the entire community around our house listening to Joe Louis fights. It was a long time before Snow Hill got its second radio, not because radios weren't popular back then, people were just too poor to afford them.

▼

My music lessons began at home. Everyone in our family played an instrument. My father played the cornet. He taught my oldest brother, Arnold, the clarinet, and my brother Clarence, the trombone. My mother, whom we called "Mur," taught my sister Consuela the piano. When I came along in 1928, my father taught me the drums. And my youngest sister, Grace, sang. We called ourselves the Lee Family Band. My father wanted to take us out on the road, but my mother was against it. We did make three appearances: in Beatrice, Alabama; in Selma, where my father was born; and on campus at Snow Hill's Wallace Buttrick Hall. Len and Cliff, my baby brothers, who were too young to play with us, stayed home with Mur. We sold tickets to those shows for fifteen cents apiece. I still have a couple at home.

When I was coming up, there was an organization in the South called New Farmers of America, which had chapters in most high schools. Future Farmers of America was its White counterpart. The statewide chapter of NFA was asked to put together a band to represent Alabama at the 1939 New York World's Fair. The nucleus of the band was culled from the school, and my father was chosen as one of the bandleaders, along with Mr. Clay, the jazzman of Snow Hill. I was the lead drummer in the band, though I was only eleven years old at the time. When people saw me onstage they'd say, "Look at that little boy up there playing drums."

We were sent to Tuskegee Institute to hone our band. Nothing could have made my father happier than to go to his alma mater with a band from Snow Hill, Alabama. We stayed there for two weeks practicing with Tuskegee's band director. I remember him telling us when we arrived that we sounded great, but we were welcome to stay anyway.

A band representing the North Carolina chapter of the New Farmers of America was invited to the Fair as well. That band was from North Carolina A&T, a college in Greensboro. The bandleader, a cornetist named Shortie Hall, had been Dizzy Gillespie's bandmaster at the Laurinburg Institute, and a great influence on Diz. The A&T band was something else! They would take those simple military songs and add a jazz beat.

When I heard the A&T band, I tried to do the same. As a strict disciplinarian, my father didn't approve of this. He'd tell me, "Play that beat straight or I'll crack you." But I would still try to sneak in a jazz beat whenever I could. I'd roll in with one, and my father would cut me a look or say, "Boy, don't you put that accent there or I'll knock you down."

Though I came from a distinguished family, as Black people living in the rural

South we were poor nonetheless. I received assistance from two Northern foundations to attend Morehouse College, but I still had to work my way through school. The summer before I left for Morehouse, I worked at a sawmill. The guys at the mill were placing bets that I wouldn't last a day. I hadn't done a lick of hard labor in my life. I did last two weeks, enough to make $37.50 to buy me some clothes for school. At the time, zoot suits were popular in Snow Hill. I bought two gabardine zoot suits, one brown, one blue. Fifteen at the ankle, thirty-two at the knee, I was sharp. I packed up and went on to Atlanta.

I got to Morehouse at two o'clock in the morning and didn't see a soul. I was up bright and early, and had my eye out for all the zoot suits to compare them to mine. Wouldn't you know, not a zoot suit on campus. This was 1947—fashion had changed on me overnight! I took those two zoot suits and packed them as far down in my trunk as I could. Consequently, I didn't have anything to wear. Other than music, that was my main concern.

I was a basketball star when I graduated at age nineteen from Snow Hill Institute. I wasn't thinking about music—I wanted to be a coach. In fact, I planned on studying physical education at Morehouse, but instead I taught myself to play the bass violin.

Actually, I started composing music back in Snow Hill. I wrote my class song at the Institute, and wrote and arranged songs for my brothers and sisters to play at home. I played the drums and flute when I was young, but I always wanted to play the trumpet, which was too close to my father's instrument, the cornet. He knew this, but he continued to bring me every instrument other than the one I wanted to play. I don't think he wanted the competition! I'd say, "Daddy, I want a trumpet." He'd say, "Boy, your teeth is not made right."

My first inspiration as a bass player was a gentleman named Jimmy Blanton, who played with Duke Ellington. I don't think many people know Jimmy Blanton. He played with Duke for maybe two years or so, and died of consumption when he was only twenty-one years old. I idolized the way he played bass. On the radio in Snow Hill I heard records by Duke Ellington, with Jimmy Blanton on bass—songs like "Body and Soul" and "Jack the Bear." Even today, no one comes near to what Blanton was on that bass violin, his tone and technique. To me, he was playing bebop ideas then, and this was back in '41.

I didn't pursue music right away at Morehouse. Hearing Charlie Parker was what led me to it. Though music was very much a part of my household—I heard all sorts, from European classical to the big bands—I didn't fall in love with any of it. It was bebop that inspired me to be a musician. It lifted me up and made me want to learn an instrument. During my summers off from Morehouse, I would go up to Chicago just to hear the music. I had a friend from Snow Hill who had moved to Chicago and stayed with him. The first summer I got a dishwashing job, but the next summer I lived off some savings and spent my time following around jazz musicians. I wasn't playing anything at the time—these were the summers of '48 and '49.

I started hanging out with a group of musicians from Atlanta and the local colleges who followed bebop. I wanted to play an instrument quick, and I knew that I could learn the bass in about six months. Morehouse didn't have any instruments, but our sister school, Spelman College, had two or three basses. I spent a lot of time over there practicing and, sure enough, in six months I had it down. I found a job playing bass right away, and soon I was earning a living as a musician. I bought my first bass from a musician who was forced to sell it 'cause he needed the money. It was made by the King Company from Ohio and I still have it today.

I played at clubs around Atlanta, from the "Ponciana," which was a pretty nice place, to rough gutbuckets like the "Peacock." Any night you could go by there and witness five or six knock-down-drag-out fights. The whole club would get torn up, but the management would put the seats back together and start all over again.

It was easy for me to go out in a community in Atlanta and meet people. In Snow Hill it had been my style to go out in the community and make friends. As small as Snow Hill was, there were divisions: My family was considered part of the elite, the leaders and teachers of the community, but the people that I hung out with were workers. My mother beat me every day after I came back from playing with the children in the community. She wanted to break me from spending time with "the bad people," as she called them, but every day I'd go right back. Even at Morehouse, the guys I hung around with were the rebels. We stayed in a dormitory called Dirty Deuce and were looked upon as outcasts.

I graduated from Morehouse in '51 and stayed in Atlanta for a year afterward playing music. I was going with a girl from Spelman named Jacquelyn Shelton whose family lived in the city. The older guys at school always told me, "Get you a girl in the city whose mom can cook a big old fine dinner on Sunday." This way you wouldn't have to starve. The last meal of the week on campus was served on Sunday at two o'clock and you got an apple and an orange to last you till Monday morning. So, I'd eat with the Sheltons on Sunday and court Jackie.

I wanted to go to Chicago to play music and Jackie and her father encouraged me. My family wasn't too happy about the idea at first. They expected me to be a schoolteacher like others in the family. I told them how determined I was to make a living as a musician, and eventually they let me be. I started playing the bass in 1950.

I left Atlanta in '52. Jackie and I got married in '54, but she didn't join me in Chicago until later. Spike was born in '57 in Atlanta. Our second son, Chris, was born in '59 in Chicago. We moved to New York shortly after.

In Chicago from '52 to '59, I met just about all the famous musicians of the time. There was a club there called the "Blue Note" that was run by a gentleman named Holdstein who had a lot of respect for the music. He presented it quite nicely. Duke Ellington played there often. I was able to meet Ellington through his right-hand man, Billy Strayhorn, a pianist and composer of great tunes like "Take the A Train," Duke's famous theme song. Duke called Strayhorn "Sweet Pea" 'cause he was the nicest man you'd ever want to meet.

It was a great thrill for me to meet Duke Ellington. I came to his hotel, and there he was in his satin robe, lounging on the bed. Strayhorn had his own trio and Duke encouraged me to play with them during that time in Chicago. Later on, when I was living in New York, I returned to Chicago to play with the folksinger Odetta at the Ravinia Summer Festival. Ellington was the headline act. His bass player, Aaron Bell, was late for the job, so Duke asked me to play with him until Aaron arrived. I played sixteen bars of "Take the A Train" before he rushed out onstage.

During this time I also had the opportunity to play with Billie Holiday, Carmen McRae, and Sarah Vaughan. There's something I found out standing on the band-stand next to these famous singers: Running through each singer's voice was a golden thread that couldn't be recorded. It's hard to describe, but it was something like a smooth hum. The most magnificent sound you'd ever want to hear was these voices in their natural state, without any amplification.

I heard Charlie Parker play in a jam session when he came through Chicago on tour. At the time, even a musical genius like Bird would have to go out on tour without a band. Headliners had to pick up musicians in every city where they were booked. This cut down costs for their management and the club owners. Ultimately it was a form of exploitation and disrespect. You couldn't perform at your best if you didn't know the cats you were playing with. This is not to put down local musicians, it's just a matter of rehearsal time and the level of musicianship that comes from working with the same people for a length of time.

▼

All the greats that I didn't get a chance to play with in Chicago, I had the opportunity to meet and hear play. I witnessed an extraordinary concert in 1948, two summers before I started playing. It was Dizzy Gillespie's big bebop band, with Charlie Parker as the soloist. Now that was some evening! There was such a spirit in those years. I guess the war was over and people were feeling a bit rich. Young people were following bebop like young folks today follow rap. People came to dance to bebop—to the music of Charlie Parker and Dizzy Gillespie—and these gigs would be advertised as dance concerts. One half of the audience would be standing near the stage watching the musicians, and the other half would be dancing to the music.

There were a few exceptional musicians in Atlanta when I was there, but they didn't stay long. That's why I had to leave Atlanta—it was not a place to grow as a musician, the jazz community wasn't challenging enough. Eventually I had to leave Chicago for the same reason. It was a great place to stay for a while and learn, but not a place to remain if you wanted to make your mark in the music world. Many fine musicians were born or spent time in Chicago, but moved on— Johnny Griffin, Gene Ammons, Sonny Stitt, and Dexter Gordon, for example. New York was the place.

There were two tenor players from Chicago, Clifford Jordan and John Gilmore, whom I played with often. The pianist Horace Silver heard them when he passed through and invited them to New York to record. Clifford and John asked me to write a song for that purpose, which I did, but Horace didn't use it. When the guys got back from New York, they told me that even though Horace didn't use the song, he needed a bass player, so why didn't I try out for his band. This was in 1957.

I did go to New York to meet Horace, but we didn't hit it off. The night after I parted company with him, I went down to a club in the Village called the "Cafe Bohemia." This was my first impression of New York. All these great men I had heard on record were there—Art Blakey, Paul Chambers, Art Taylor—but they were looking kind of raggedy like they didn't have a dime. I couldn't believe it. I said to myself, Wait a minute, is this me? What's out here to aspire to? The musicians would get onstage and jam for a bit, then go off. The audience was sitting around talking, almost ignoring them. I walked out of the club, and went on back to Chicago.

When I came back, I stopped in at Hall's Restaurant, a musicians' hangout. I sat down next to some of the guys and they started joking with me—"Have you seen Bill? Naw, we haven't seen him, maybe he went to New York." Finally I said, "I wasn't ready to go this time, but mark my words, I'm going back."

I did just that in '59. Something happened that gave me the determination to leave Chicago for good. There was a joint called the "Southern" on South Park and Forty-seventh Street, where the greats played. New York musicians were booked there all the time. I happened to go once on an off night. There were two gentlemen standing at the door looking in. I overheard them say, "There's nobody's here tonight but those old local guys." I went home and packed my bags.

I had met Odetta and other folksingers in Chicago and I was working off and on with them. This helped me make the move to New York. Odetta was recording and touring often at the time, and I would take these jobs when there were no jazz gigs. I learned much about presentation from folk musicians. The musicians and singers who play this type of music may not be the greatest achievers on their instruments, but they present their material well, and make an audience feel that they're glad to be there and glad the audience is there. They stand up in front of large audiences and perform with little accompaniment. On some gigs I played there would be two musicians on the stage in front of an audience of ten thousand people.

I identified with folk music because it was similar to the music that I had heard at home. Making this connection did a lot for me. I began to respect and think deeper about the music that I heard the blues singers and old folks sing back home. Listening to folksingers gave me confidence that the music I had witnessed at home had artistic validity. I began writing operas that drew on this music. I wrote my first, *The Depot*, in 1965.

When I got to New York I lugged my bass all over town jamming, just as I had done in Chicago. I went to places like the "Five Spot," where Philly Jo Jones would be playing with Jimmy Garrison, who later became John Coltrane's bassist. Jimmy and I started playing together and he threw some gigs my way. I played with Philly Jo Jones whenever Jimmy couldn't make it. From there I went on to meet and play with more people.

There was a jazz community in New York that kept musicians in touch with each other, much more so then than now. Musicians would get off their gigs and go to "Birdland" to jam. On Monday nights there were sessions for aspiring musicians. Young gentlemen at the peak of their instruments, like trumpeter Freddie

Hubbard and tenor saxophonist Wayne Shorter, were playing there then. It's too bad that so few of these sessions were recorded.

Some of the best postbebop music I heard in the early '60s was trumpeter Art Farmer playing with Benny Golson. Guys were changing their styles left and right. Freddie Hubbard was changing his style. Before he had been playing like Clifford Brown, then he broke through a barrier and came up with a completely new style of playing the trumpet. Young guys out here today, like Terence Blanchard, are children of Freddie Hubbard.

By 1966, I was working frequently as a studio musician. I was recruited by Columbia Records and John Hammond, who had heard me play with Odetta. I was still making gigs with her at the time, and naturally one day a conflict presented itself. I had made a commitment to play with Odetta on a day that the studio called me to work. They weren't too pleased that I chose to honor my commitment to Odetta. This began a chilly period between me and the studios. Shortly afterward, John Hammond called to ask me if I played Fender bass. I told him that I didn't and that I had no plans to do so. That was the last time I was called by a studio.

Bass players were worried that we'd be forced to learn Fender bass, that our instruments were being rendered obsolete. Some went out and bought Fender basses. Others of us who had no interest in electric music formed a group called Professionals Unlimited, which included Bob Cunningham, Reggie Workman, Chris White, Lyle Atkinson, Alex Blake, Herbert Brown, and lesser-known bass players who had earned fabulous salaries downtown doing studio work.

At first we were purely a professional organization devoted to saving and investing money. Somebody suggested that we start playing together, so we did. I was nominated to write for the group. In 1968, we performed at Town Hall. We did excerpts from my operas *One Mile East* and *The Depot* at this concert. Some of the original people involved became uninterested. I went on to found and manage a group called the New York Bass Violin Choir. The Choir included many great bassists, including Milt Hinton, Ron Carter, Richard Davis, and the late Sam Jones. Michael Fleming, our youngest member, was Bill Nunn's bass coach for *Mo' Better Blues*. My sisters Consuela and Grace also joined the Choir, on piano and vocals.

We were well received on the East Coast college circuit. We got as far south as Hampton, Virginia, where at Hampton Institute, in 1973, we performed *The Depot*

Maestro Bill Lee.

▼

Photo by J. Robert Gibeau.

in its entirety. The Choir played as a group from '68 to '76, occasionally getting together after that. In 1970, I founded, along with Bill Hardman and Billy Higgins, the Brass Company, a ten-piece combination of brass instruments, bass, and drums. We performed together through the mid-'70s. And in 1971, along with my brothers and sisters, I founded the Descendants of Mike & Phoebe, a family group. Consuela and I did the composing and arranging for the band, and we performed a number of college concerts before disbanding a few years later.

During these years it became more important for me to develop and perform with my own organizations rather than go downtown to work for someone else. Many musicians I knew were trying to do the same. From 1970 to 1975, I was affiliated as a producer with Strata-East, an independent record company owned by jazz musicians. The company was run by pianist Stanley Cowell and trumpet player Charles Toliver. At one time they had a catalogue of close to forty musicians. Clifford Jordan was one of their mainstays.

When you recorded an album for a major label back then, you would never get to own your master tape. The entire recording process was a mystery to most of us. We thought you needed fifty thousand dollars to press a record and market it, which isn't true. Strata-East was an important company because it showed jazz musicians that records could be produced and recorded for under five thousand dollars.

My first wife, Jacquelyn Shelton Lee, passed on October 28, 1976. I don't have much recollection of what happened between '76 and '78—I was meditating and plotting a new direction. I met my current wife, Susan Kaplan Lee, in '78 while playing with Barry Harris at a club called "Brodie's" in Manhattan. From that union we have one child, Arnold Tone Kaplan Lee, already a master drummer at four years of age.

Spike graduated from Morehouse in 1978, and went on to NYU film school. I got a grant the same year to compose for a large orchestra that Susan and I had formed called the Natural Spiritual Orchestra. We put on a concert in '82. Many musicians who played in our first concert with the Orchestra are now working for me when we record the scores for Spike's features.

I started composing scores for Spike's student films in his second year. Spike always said having original music distinguished his films from the others because most students just used records. I had the opportunity to call upon some great musicians to assist us. They were cooperative and worked for the little Spike had to pay them at the time.

The first student film we scored was *Sarah* in 1981. Spike adapted *Sarah* from a short story written by another writer. I always thought he was capable of writing his own stories, and since that time that's what he's done. For *Sarah* we used a quartet: I played bass, James Spaulding was on alto and flute, Sonelius Smith was on piano, and Leroy Williams was on drums. In the opening credits of *Sarah*, there's an image of a man leading a mule and plow that appears along with the production company name, "Forty Acres and a Mule." I wrote a theme by the same name that plays over that image. I thought Spike should have held on to that theme and used it to open all his films to come, but he didn't agree.

We did Spike's thesis film, *Joe's Bed-Stuy Barbershop: We Cut Heads*, in 1982. I played bass, Ted Dunbar was on acoustic guitar, Micky Tucker was on piano, George Coleman was on tenor, and Joe Chambers was on drums. *Joe's* won a Student Academy Award, but I thought it deserved even more attention than it was given. The Academy had no idea that Spike was coming from such a strong background, one that would sustain him as he continued to do greater work. I doubt if they knew Spike was my son or the great-grandson of the founder of Snow Hill Institute. Had they investigated a bit, I think more to-do would have been made of the award.

There were four years between *Joe's* and Spike's first feature film, *She's Gotta Have It*. I was able to select music for the score of *She's Gotta Have It* from compositions I had written between '82 and '86. "Nola's Theme," the score's main theme, was adapted from "Ye Little Old Folk's Children's Concert Waltz," which is included in my opera *One Mile East*.

I enjoyed *School Daze* immensely. During the production period in '87, I was back and forth all the time from my home in Brooklyn to the set in Atlanta. In addition to composing the score, I was musical director—I supervised the recording and was on hand when Spike filmed the musical numbers.

School Daze's main theme, "One Little Acorn," didn't come in until late. I must credit my first opera, *The Depot*, for giving birth to "One Little Acorn." The music was inspired by the words "from one little acorn there grew a great oak tree, and it spread its mighty, mighty branches forth," which are part of a preacher's sermon in *The Depot*'s big church scene.

The main theme of *Do the Right Thing*, which we called "Mookie," was inspired by an earlier piece of music of mine, "Grown Folks Conversation." The character Smiley in *Do the Right Thing* reminds me of Crazy George, a weird character I

▼

used to see around my neighborhood. Smiley's musical theme was inspired by "Suite for Crazy George," a large-scale piece I wrote for the Brass Company. Even though I refer to earlier pieces, the majority of the music that makes up the scores is new.

Quite a bit of music that I have composed over the years has never been performed. No one commissioned me to write this music—I just felt it had to be written at the time. Looking back, I see that it gave me the opportunity to practice writing large-scale pieces and those with many types of instrumentation, so it's been beneficial—certainly better than if I had written nothing because no one commissioned the work, or given up because of the slim chance that any of the music I was writing at the time would be heard. Besides, if I hadn't written this music, I wouldn't be as selective as I am today in composing and arranging.

The same thing goes for my literary writing. I've written two unpublished novels. One, called *Marriage by Mail*, is based on my relationship with my first wife, Jackie, and the other deals with jazz musicians. When I first tried my hand at fiction, I had no inhibitions at all about subject matter. I wrote anything and everything that I could imagine. I just had to write this stuff out. Now, with a better idea of what works and what doesn't, I can be more selective.

When it comes to composing a score, you have to let the movie and each individual scene dictate the mood and flavor of the music. Spike has a good sense of this. In fact, I consider Spike to be a jazz musician. He didn't practice an instrument to develop his expression of it, but he has the sensibility. Like a musician, he has a good ear and can remember music. Spike can give me an example of how he wants a song to sound and where he wants it in the film, and it turns out to be just the right thing.

I think of the scores as a joint effort. Spike feeds me information about tempo and feeling, like "This theme should build slowly," or "This one should have a somber feeling." They're all good suggestions. The challenge is to bring your audience as close as possible to the idea you want to get across, without sitting them down and telling them flat out what they're supposed to feel.

I approach a score as a suite of music, so it can serve as background for the film but also stand on its own and be listenable without the visuals. When I compose, I alternate tempos and keys as often as appropriate, so the audience doesn't tire of listening to the themes that repeat throughout the film. Each time the audience hears a theme it should be an enjoyable experience. When the composer/arranger doesn't change key and tempo, monotony sets in. The audience gets tired, and doesn't even know why.

I can't always wait until the rough cut of a film is complete before I begin composing the score. At the rate Spike turns out films, there isn't time. I go ahead and write songs in keys that don't repeat themselves. Sometimes I have to fiddle around for the right key for a song, or other times it will come to me as a complete piece of music. Often when I'm out of the house, away from paper and pencil, music comes to me. Later, when I try to reproduce it, I find the music has passed through. It's gone with the wind. I'm accustomed to that now. You don't capture it all, you leave some to the spirits.

Once I write a song, I live with it for a few days and consider all its possibilities —all the ways I can embellish a particular melody. After I've tried the song as many ways as I can think of, I work it out on the piano and put it on paper. The next step is the orchestration of the song. I must distribute the musical ideas in the melody, supporting parts, and rhythmic parts to each instrument in the orchestra, and commit them to score paper. Here is where I have to draw upon my knowledge of musical instruments. A French horn, for example, has more flexibility than a trombone, so I give my French horn a few more notes to play. I give the trombone a basic harmony part. The tuba will be my bass, so I give it a supporting part to my trombones, and so on.

I have a lot more options in distributing parts to the violin section, because there's so much that I can do with them. I can give the entire section one long note to hold or have one violinist play a single-line melody. For the score of *Mo' Better Blues*, I plan on having fifty-six strings: sixteen first and sixteen second violins (the firsts usually play melody), twelve violas, and twelve cellos. The strings are light instruments, so for volume and strength I have to duplicate their parts.

Once the orchestration is complete, I hum it out. I ask myself, Does it sound interesting, does it swing? Most important is whether the blend of instruments sounds natural. Are the accents natural for musicians to play? Usually what disturbs the musician will disturb the listener. That's why I try to surround myself with great musicians, because they help me judge. If a transition is clumsy, we'll discuss it, and change it so the notes flow as naturally as possible.

Once I have a piece written and orchestrated, I bring it to a copyist, who copies each instrument's part over on a separate sheet of music paper. This is quite a job, if you think about an orchestra of fifty to one hundred pieces. Once the music is copied, we're ready to rehearse and record. The first time I rehearse a song with the orchestra is really the first time I hear it as a complete piece of music.

Some composers claim they can look at a score and hear an entire orchestra in their heads, but I'm not one of them. I consider that to be some feat. I hear an individual part or a section of instruments by playing it out on the piano. I stick close to a piano when I'm writing. If I write away from the piano, there's the danger that I might rely on arrangements that I've done before, and use them over again. For me, each score is a new experience. Each song demands a new balance between instruments, new overtones, and a new approach. So, as you may guess, my writing process is a slow one. I take my time.

To pursue a jazz career, to be a jazz musician, calls for a special dedication. Once you choose to play an instrument, it's a total commitment. I believe that there are not many things that you can do along with it—the spirit may get up and find another place to dwell. I've seen it happen too many times. Great musicians get caught up in day jobs, and they just seem to dry up. I saw this often in Chicago. When men were pressured by their families to get nine-to-five jobs, or to limit their playing to the weekends, there was no place for the spirit to dwell. It had to get up and find a more dedicated home.

All of my children are artists. Their love for music and their ear for music are good guiding points for anything they do in their lives. Music is so basic—there's either a right note or a wrong note. If you play two notes and they clash, it hurts your ears. A musician learns to tell right from wrong, he learns to trust his intuition. Get the rhythm, and that'll lead you to the truth.

Bleek.

▼

The music teachers *(from left):* Michael Fleming, bass; Donald Harrison, tenor/soprano saxophone;

Terence Blanchard, trumpet; and Bill Lee, bass/piano.

▼

Giant, you couldn't manage a deli.

▼

When you hear Denzel and Wesley, you're really listening to Terence Blanchard *(right)* and Branford Marsalis *(left)*.

▼

Going over the music with Branford Marsalis *(on saxophone)*, Kenny Kirkland *(at the piano)*, my father, Jeff Watts *(in the Pirates cap)*, and Terence Blanchard *(on trumpet)*.

▼

"People are convinced that jazz is just some magic thing that happens with Negroes. We just wake up with horns in our mouths. But to play what we play, you have to be a supreme musician. The art form requires it. It requires the discipline of a classical musician, the emotional feeling that any good musician should bring to his music, and knowledge of the blues. You must have the ability to create melody on the spur of the moment, which is what improvisation is all about. Musicians who are best at improvisation are those who can create melody."—BRANFORD MARSALIS

▼

Going over ''Pop Top 40'' with Terence: ''We were shooting a scene one day, and I, as usual, was at the video monitor watching Denzel. The camera started rolling. I must have had a worried look on my face. Denzel stopped in the middle of the take. 'What's the matter with you, man?' he said. 'You look like a nervous mother. Get away from me, man, you're making me nervous!' ''—TERENCE BLANCHARD

▼

Reviewing the script with Denzel and Terence: "I made a videotape of myself playing Bleek's trumpet parts, and sent it to Denzel in California so he'd have something to work with before he came to New York to begin rehearsals. It would have taken too long for me to show him every note and every scale, so I had him memorize the fingerings to each song.

"Denzel has a good ear. Soon he could play the melodies and he would try to play along with the track, note for note. When he made a mistake, his natural tendency was to correct it. But once he stopped to make the correction, the playback track would get ahead of him. So we had to backtrack. I had Denzel put the trumpet down, listen to the track, and learn to 'sing' his part. Once he memorized a song this way, it was easier for him to follow the playback track. He could press any valve on the trumpet, even if it wasn't the right one. And as long as he pressed with confidence, and in sync, while blowing into the horn, his execution was believable."

—TERENCE BLANCHARD

▼

MO'
BETTER
BLUES

Two-tone joints: The musicians in *Mo' Better Blues* emulate and dress like their heroes from other eras,

especially bebop musicians of the '40s and '50s.

▼

Shadow.

▼

Walkin' bass: "I went to my coach Mike's gigs to watch him play. He took me to check out other bassists. I was able to meet cats like Ron Carter and hang out with them a bit. Unless you're a bandleader like Ron Carter, it seems to me that bass players are humble characters, because they're always in the background. They are like offensive linemen: unassuming players who occupy a difficult and crucial position.

"The front men, the sax and trumpet players, get to rest. They come out, play, and all the women go crazy. Then they go back, chill, and stand pretty holding their horns. But a bass player plays from beginning to end, every time. It's dogged work. And you've got this big thing to lug around. Not only is it big, but it's delicate. Bass playing is just a hell of a sacrifice."—BILL NUNN

▼

Bottom Hammer and Rhythm Jones: "Spike had me go to music rehearsals along with the other guys in the band, even though there was no reason for me to be there. I guess I was there to lend some musical moral support. On one occasion the guys were preparing to run through a piece for the hundredth time, and I said, 'Stop, don't do it, you're killing me.' I was kidding, of course.

"It would have been easy for me, as a professional musician, to condescend to them as musicians, just as it would be easy for them as actors to ridicule my acting. I have no experience, I've never taken classes. It was just as difficult for me to turn my character on and off, or place myself in a scene given that everything is filmed out of sequence, as it was for them to get a sound out of their instruments."—JEFF WATTS

MO'
BETTER
BLUES

▼

Dressing room: "The songs the band played on film were either very fast and hard or they were ballads. We needed a tune or two in the middle, a tune to communicate more of the sensuality of jazz—where the groove is apparent, but there's a lot of emotion and blues feeling in conjunction with the groove. Hopefully this type of tune will show up elsewhere in the film, in the score or among the incidental music."—JEFF WATTS

▼

"Denzel, Spike, and I went to see a Mike Tyson fight in Atlantic City about four months before the shoot. This was the first time I met Denzel. On the drive down, I let him hold my horn so he could get familiar with it. I said, 'It has to become a part of you, you can't look like you're afraid of the instrument.' He took it out of the case and held it all the way down."—TERENCE BLANCHARD

▼

Ladies and gentlemen, my name is Bleek Gilliam.

▼

Listening to the playback of ''Pop Top 40'': ''When the crew was setting up for the next shot, Denzel had his headphones on reviewing the musical number. He'd go back on stage, often before the other principal actors. And while the extras were taking their place on the set, he'd fiddle around with the trumpet to get used to playing in front of people. While everybody else was talking and running around, Denzel was alone on the stage, pacing around with his headphones and his trumpet.''—TERENCE BLANCHARD

▼

MO'
BETTER
MUSIC

"After the shoot, I went back on the road with Branford Marsalis. Branford started introducing me on stage as

'Rhythm Jones.' I bet a bunch of people out here think that's my real name."—JEFF WATTS

▼

Left Hand, late again.

▼

Seduction.

▾

MO'
BETTER
BLUES

"I loved the music scenes, but half the time I was nervous as hell. As an actor, every time I do a scene, my

stomach drops, my heart drops. Once I open my mouth, I'm fine. If you were sitting next to me, you'd never

know I was going through changes. Got a scene today, nervous level number one. Shit, it's a music scene. Do I

know the music? Nervous level number two. Oh shit, do I have the fingering right? Nervous level number three.

Damn, all the extras are out there just waiting to see if I can really play this horn, nervous level number four.

Once they rolled the playback, I was okay. In fact, it would pump me up. I'd say, 'Yeah, let's ride this baby.' "

—WESLEY SNIPES

▼

Indigo teaching her third-grade class to sing ''M & N,'' composed by Bill Lee. Unfortunately, the scene didn't

make the final cut. No matter how much you like a given scene, if it doesn't serve the film as a whole, it's got

to go.

▼

Bleek composes "Pop Top 40": "In rehearsals with the band and Spike, Denzel wanted to know what made Bleek tick. He felt his character was somewhat like Wynton Marsalis, because both play traditionally based music. But unlike Wynton, Bleek doesn't have an outlet for making money, playing concert hall gigs or classical music. Is Bleek a hypocrite for loving jazz and refusing to play other music? Is he a dinosaur?

"Tradition is important for reasons other than to re-create the past. When an actor studies Shakespeare, it's not because he wants to do Shakespeare for the rest of his life, it's for the use of language. It's just more information to draw upon. Having a concern for tradition doesn't mean that you merely want to copy something that was done thirty years ago, but expand what you're doing today."—JEFF WATTS

▼

In the studio, rappin' to "Pop Top 40": "I suggested to Denzel that he listen to as much music as he could get his hands on. I directed him specifically to musicians whose work related to Bleek, the character, his one-sidedness—Miles Davis, Thelonious Monk, and John Coltrane."—TERENCE BLANCHARD

▼

The recording session for "Harlem Blues." Raymond Jones, here with Cynda, produced the song. Raymond has written, arranged, and produced songs for *School Daze, Do the Right Thing,* and now *Mo' Better Blues.* A while back, Raymond's father gave him a book of songs by W. C. Handy, "the Father of the Blues." He liked the lyrics to "Harlem Blues," so he put a new melody to it.

▼

"Hanging out with Terence and the musicians, checking out their life style, was an education for me. And, the

trumpet? Well, it was enjoyable, it was painful, it was humbling, it was hard, and hopefully it was rewarding.

Just try to make a sound out of the damn thing! It's got to be one of the most, if not *the* most, difficult

instruments to play. I tinkle on the piano, now and again, but the trumpet is unforgiving."

—DENZEL WASHINGTON

The Shadow Henderson Quartet: "In the '20s, there was one way of holding the horn; in the '30s, there was another. In the '40s, the less you moved, the more precise you were. In the '50s, it was the thing to stand up front and be cool. In the '60s, there was a lot of moving around and it was very emotional. John Coltrane would get on his knees sometimes. In the modern era, most guys hold their horn to the center. Wesley ended up combining eras."—DONALD HARRISON

▼

"Spike gave me a tape of 'Harlem Blues' when I was cast as Clarke, but he was adamant that I not settle on

a style for the song because Raymond, as the producer, likes to work along with the singer to arrive at one.

"First we recorded the entire song. Then we recorded each line separately, with Raymond and Spike giving

directions like, 'You see Bleek walking into the club now. You're supposed to be feeling a lot of love, so let's

try it with a lot of love here.' So, I would sing each line, ten to fifteen times, until we got it right. Sometimes

we had to modify my Middle Western twang—I guess it's the hillbilly in me. My father calls it Blackabilly."

—CYNDA WILLIAMS

▼

Bleek's chops are gone.

▼

"Sing Soweto," the song Bleek plays on the Brooklyn Bridge, was written by Terence Blanchard, in memory of the children who were killed in the Sharpeville Massacre in South Africa.

▼

CBS Records, which released the soundtrack album, made up mock album covers for Bleek Gilliam, which we used as props in his loft. I chose the titles: *Song of Solomon, Bleek Street,* and *(not pictured) Pitter Patter* and *Flatbush Avenue.*

▼

mo'
B E T T E R
SUGGESTED
LISTENING

For those unfamiliar with jazz, some suggestions of must-have sounds from the musicians who helped me on this project.

—Spike Lee

B R A N F O R D   M A R S A L I S

Miles Davis	*Kind of Blue*
Miles Davis	*Relaxin' with the Miles Davis Quintet*
John Coltrane	*Soultrane*
Charlie Parker	*April in Paris*
Charlie Parker	*Charlie Parker with Strings*
Lester Young	*Lester Swings*
Clifford Brown	*Clifford Brown with Strings*
Nat King Cole and George Shearing	*Nat King Cole Sings, George Shearing Plays*
Billie Holiday	*Songs for Distingué Lovers*
Ben Webster	*Soulville*
Sonny Rollins	*Way Out West*

J E F F   W A T T S

Thelonious Monk	*Thelonious Monk Plays Duke Ellington*
Miles Davis	*Kind of Blue*
John Coltrane	*Crescent*
Charlie Parker	*The Complete Savoy Studio Sessions/Charlie Parker*
Duke Ellington	*Any album by Ellington*
Louis Armstrong	*Satchmo at Symphony Hall*
Billie Holiday	*The Original Decca Masters*
Ben Webster	*Ballads*
Ornette Coleman	*New York Is Now*
Sonny Rollins	*On Impulse!*

T E R E N C E   B L A N C H A R D

Ella Fitzgerald and Louis Armstrong	*Ella Fitzgerald and Louis Armstrong*
Miles Davis	*Porgy and Bess*
Miles Davis	*Live at the Plugged Nickel*
Clifford Brown	*Clifford Brown with Strings*
Clifford Brown and Max Roach	*Study in Brown*
Charlie Parker	*The Complete Savoy Studio Sessions/Charlie Parker*
Thelonious Monk	*Alone in San Francisco*
Thelonious Monk	*Thelonious Monk Plays Duke Ellington*
John Coltrane	*Coltrane*
Ben Webster and Harry "Sweets" Edison	*Ben and "Sweets"*

M A X   R O A C H

Long live the music of:

Scott Joplin, King Oliver, Louis Armstrong, Sidney Bechet, Fletcher Henderson, Duke Ellington, James Reese Europe, Jimmy Lunceford, Benny Carter, Chick Webb, Baby Dodds, Papa Jo Jones, Kenny Clarke, Art Tatum, Bud Powell, Teddy Wilson, Willie "the Lion" Smith, Coleman Hawkins, Lester Young, Charlie Parker, Thelonious Monk, Dizzy Gillespie, J. J. Johnson, Sonny Rollins, John Coltrane, Bill Lee, and then some!!!

Any recordings of:

Mahalia Jackson, Blind Lemon Jefferson, Huddie Ledbetter, Billie Holiday, Ella Fitzgerald, Aretha Franklin, Bessie Smith, Ray Charles, Stevie Wonder, and Otis Redding.

mo'
BETTER
SCRIPT

I started taking notes on *Mo' Better Blues* in December 1988, began the first draft on April 1, 1989, and completed it on April 16. That's fifteen days writing the actual script—about the time it takes me to complete a solid first draft. I did make more revisions on *Mo' Better Blues* than on any of my other scripts to date. All the revisions are included in the script that follows.

Ask your parents which child they like best, and they'll tell you "all of my children." I like all of my films. I can't watch *She's Gotta Have It* anymore, but without that film I wouldn't be where I am today. How about *School Daze?* We got our share of negative reviews from those who probably never knew Black colleges existed before. But I bet in the years to come, with thanks to videocassettes, the film will be better appreciated.

Do the Right Thing was that rare case where everything clicked—New York City's 1989 mayoral race: Democrat David Dinkins (Black) upset four-term Mayor

Ed Koch (White) in the primary, then Republican Rudy Giuliani (White) in the general election; the racially motivated murder of a young Black man, Yusef Hawkins, in the streets of Bensonhurst—it was the right film at the right time. Now, *Mo' Better Blues.*

As I write more scripts, I hope to write less and less. By that I mean, to not include shit that's just gonna be cut down the line. I've got to work on that—letting the images speak. Another thing, my grandmother is too through with all the profanity in my films.

Profanity is why we couldn't use the title *Love Supreme*, based on the title of Coltrane's famous album. John's widow, Alice Coltrane, is very religious. To woo Alice, I cut out the profanity—curse by curse, motherfucker by motherfucker. I sent Alice three different versions of the script. The last one was practically profanity-free. My grandmother would have been proud. I got a call from Alice's lawyer, who said that as long as one profane word remained, Mrs. Coltrane wouldn't grant us the title. That was it, end of discussion. The next day, all the "motherfuckers" went back in.

Another thing, will I be burned in effigy for my female characters? Who knows. I'm working on that also. Shit, I got a lot to fucking work on.

S p i k e   L e e

mo'
BETTER
BLUES

Revised Second Draft—August 28, 1989

Forty Acres and a Mule Filmworks

Ya-Dig Sho-Nuff

By Any Means Necessary

Brooklyn, New York

1 **EXT:** *BROOKLYN STREET—DAY 1969*
Four kids are yelling at the top of their lungs.
TYRONE
Bleek. Yo, Bleek. Yo, Bleek. Come on out to play. Come on out to play.
JOE
We're wasting time on him.
ANGLE—WINDOW
LILLIAN, a middle-aged woman, sticks her head out of the fourth-floor brownstone window to see what all the commotion is about.
LILLIAN
Boys! Boys! Please be quiet.
CLOSE—TYRONE
TYRONE
Sorry, Mrs. Gilliam. We want to know if Bleek can come out?
CLOSE—LILLIAN
LILLIAN
I understand that, but your noise has to stop.
She pulls her head back in.

2 **INT:** *BIG STOP'S LIVING ROOM—DAY*
WE DOLLY BACK as Lillian leads us into the living room where BLEEK, eight years old, is practicing his scales on a trumpet. His father, affectionately known as BIG STOP, sits in front of a TV watching a baseball game with the sound off.
LILLIAN
Bleek, didn't I tell you to tell your hoodlum friends not to come around here?
BIG STOP
Aw, Gem! Leave the boy alone.
BLEEK
Can I go outside now?
LILLIAN
Not until you finish your practice.
BLEEK
What about then?
LILLIAN
We'll see.
BIG STOP
Let the boy be a boy, have some fun.
LILLIAN
He could be a bum for all you care. Running the streets with those wild kids.
TYRONE (OS)
Yo, Bleek! Yo, Bleek! Come on out.
LILLIAN
That chile is gonna drive me up a wall. Go tell him to go home.
BLEEK
Mommy, you don't let me do anything.

3 **EXT:** *STREET—DAY*
   CLOSE—WINDOW

> **BLEEK**
> Yo, Ty. What did I tell ya about that stuff?

CLOSE—TYRONE

> **TYRONE**
> Are you coming out or not?

CLOSE—BLEEK

> **BLEEK**
> When I'm done.

CLOSE—TYRONE

> **TYRONE**
> Done what?

CLOSE—BLEEK

> **BLEEK**
> Finish my lessons.

ANGLE—KIDS

> **SAM**
> Forget him.

> **TYRONE**
> We're going.

CLOSE—BLEEK

> **BLEEK**
> I'll see ya later.

ANGLE—KIDS

> **TYRONE**
> I'm glad my moms ain't like your moms. My moms lets me do whatever I want, when I want.

> **JOE**
> Me too!

> **LOUIS**
> Yeah!

CLOSE—BLEEK

> **BLEEK**
> I said I'll see ya later.

CLOSE—TYRONE & SAM

> **TYRONE**
> We'll see you later . . . MAMA'S BOY!

> **SAM**
> SISSY!

The kids take off down the block.

CLOSE—TYRONE

Pain is all over his face as he watches his friends run down the block having *big fun*. From his prison window, they are having the time of their lives.

> **LILLIAN (OS)**
> Bleek, get your butt out of that window.

4 **INT:** *LIVING ROOM—DAY*

Bleek stands in the living room with his mouth all stuck out.

BLEEK

Mommy, I never get to play with my friends. Now they call me a sissy.
I ain't no sissy.

LILLIAN

Don't pay those fools no mind.

BIG STOP

A SISSY!

BLEEK

I'm sick and tired of this trumpet. I hate the trumpet.

Big Stop looks at his son, gets up from in front of the TV and goes to him.

BIG STOP

Don't say that, Bleek. You'll have a lot of time to play with your
friends. Don't hate that instrument, it's also your friend. We'll go to a
ballgame. Just me and you. I'll make it up to you.

CLOSE—BLEEK

BLEEK

I still hate it.

Bleek sticks the trumpet into his mouth.

SMASH CUT TO:

5   **INT:** *"BENEATH THE UNDERDOG" STAGE—NIGHT*
CLOSE—TRUMPET IN MOUTH—TWENTY YEARS LATER

Bleek is onstage at "Beneath the Underdog." It is one of the most popular jazz
clubs in Manhattan. The smoke-filled club is packed and Bleek is killing, he's
firing as he heads his BLEEK QUINTET. On the small stage with him is RHYTHM
JONES on drums, LEFT HAND LACEY on piano, BOTTOM HAMMER on bass,
and SHADOW HENDERSON on tenor and soprano sax.

CLOSE—SHADOW

Shadow looks directly at Bleek and begins to take his solo.

CLOSE—BLEEK

Bleek gives him a look that says plainly, "Keep it short."

CLOSE—SHADOW

Shadow winks at Bleek and moves upstage. He is definitely playing to and for the
audience.

ANGLE—BLEEK

Bleek walks offstage and stands next to GIANT, a smallish man who is dressed
very sharp. He's the manager of the band; slung over his shoulder is a portable
phone.

BLEEK

There he goes again.

GIANT

He's a chucker. He comes off the bench shooting. You'd never see no
passes from him. A selfish ballplayer.

CLOSE—SHADOW

Shadow is still playing away.

BLEEK (OS)

He's only out for himself.

GIANT (OS)

Bleek, sooner or later you gotta do something quick. It's your team.

It's your band. You're the coach. Fire his ass.

CLOSE—BLEEK

BLEEK

I know.

ANGLE—STAGE

Bleek walks back onstage and up to the microphone and interrupts Shadow's solo.

BLEEK

Shadow Henderson on tenor sax. Let's hear it for him. Ladies and gentlemen, Shadow Henderson.

CLOSE—SHADOW

Shadow takes a bow, then smiles at Bleek.

ANGLE—STAGE

The other members of the band exchange looks, "What's going on?" Bleek nods at Rhythm and on the beat, the band comes back in together for the final chorus of the song.

CLOSE—BLEEK

He smiles back at Shadow.

ANGLE—STAGE

The song ends.

ANGLE—CROWD

The audience enthusiastically applauds.

CLOSE—BLEEK'S MOUTH

In SLOW MOTION the mouthpiece comes out of his mouth.

CLOSE—BLEEK—IN REAL TIME

BLEEK

Thank you. This brings us to the end of our first set. On drums . . .

CLOSE—RHYTHM—SLOW MOTION—DOLLY

BLEEK (OS)

Rhythm Jones.

CLOSE—BLEEK

BLEEK

Left Hand Lacey . . .

CLOSE—LEFT HAND LACEY—SLOW MOTION—DOLLY

BLEEK (OS)

on piano.

ANGLE—BLEEK

BLEEK

Bottom Hammer on bass.

CLOSE—BOTTOM—SLOW MOTION—DOLLY

CLOSE—BLEEK

BLEEK

And Shadow Henderson on tenor and soprano sax.

CLOSE—SHADOW—SLOW MOTION—DOLLY

He takes the biggest bow, the crowd responds with cheers.

ANGLE—STAGE

BLEEK

My name is Bleek Gilliam and *we* thank you for coming, because you didn't have to come. You coulda stayed home and watched Arsenio Hall.

The audience laughs.

                              BLEEK

Just kidding. Seriously, I like the brother. God bless him . . . So we
do appreciate it. We do thank you.

ANGLE—AUDIENCE
They applaud as the band leaves the stage.
ANGLE—STAGE

                              BLEEK

We'll be back after a little break, so please make our beautiful
waitresses work, tell 'em they look good and give 'em a tip. We all got
to make a livin'. Here's Butterbean!

BUTTERBEAN, a dark, round man, is the M.C. for the club; he's a comic/blues
singer. Butterbean cracks on Bleek while they're leaving the stage.

5A   **INT:** *UNDERDOG BACKSTAGE—NIGHT*
     ANGLE—BACKSTAGE—HAND-HELD—LONG TRAVELING SHOT
     WE FOLLOW Giant as he hands towels to the guys as they go to their dressing
     room. All of them are soaking wet.
     CLOSE—BLEEK
     The stage smile that was on Bleek's face has since disappeared.

5B   **INT:** *UNDERDOG DRESSING ROOM—NIGHT*
     Bleek, the last one in, slams the door.

                              BLEEK

Shadow, when are you gonna stop grandstanding?

                             SHADOW

The people eat it up.

                              BLEEK

That ain't 'bout nuthin' but some ego shit. You taking all day and
night for your solos. Cut that shit out.

                             SHADOW

Do I tell you what to play and for how long?

                              BLEEK

Hell no. You ain't me. You ain't the leader.

                           LEFT HAND

Bleek, he sounds good.

                              GIANT

Shut up! Who asked you?

                           LEFT HAND

Nobody asked me.

                              GIANT

That's what I thought. Shut the fuck up.

                             SHADOW

Midget, who asked you?

                              GIANT

Giant is the name.

                             SHADOW

Excuse me . . . Midget.

                              BLEEK

Yo! Yo!
Everyone chills.

BLEEK

Shadow, do me a favor, do us all a favor. Do as I say . . .

He looks at him.

BLEEK

. . . or you could always quit.

SHADOW

I could quit.

The room falls deathly quiet, nobody is saying anything, just looking, until . . .

GIANT

Left Hand.

LEFT HAND

What?

GIANT

Your moms is so old she has powdered milk coming out of her titties.

The guys explode with laughs, the tension is broken.

LEFT HAND

Midget, your moms is so old, she has Jesus' beeper number.

GIANT

Your mother has one pubic hair on her vagina with a curler on it. Does VO5 commercials.

On cue, everyone jumps in and it's a "dozens" free-for-all.

5C **INT: *"BENEATH THE UNDERDOG" STAGE—DAY***

Butterbean is going through his routine. He has a sophisticated country vibe about him. A unique blend of the Bayou and Uptown, it's a strange and funny mix. Butterbean keeps getting bothered by a heckler, STERLING, a well-dressed Black man. He tries to ignore him, but the guy won't stop. Finally Butterbean has had it; he walks over to the guy.

BUTTERBEAN

Sir, why are you fuckin' with me?

STERLING

Why? Cuz you're so country. So Bama. I didn't know niggers like you still existed. This is the 1990s. We're out of slavery.

BUTTERBEAN

Where are you from?

STERLING

The Upper East Side.

BUTTERBEAN

What the fuck is the Upper East Side?

STERLING

Manhattan, New York City. The Big Apple.

BUTTERBEAN

What's your name?

STERLING

Sterling Randolph.

BUTTERBEAN

Sterling Randolph, my name is Butterbean, and I'm from a little country town called *Two Seconds Fresh Offa Nigger's Ass*. Keep fuckin' with me and I'm gonna be homesick.

The crowd roars.

STERLING

Go back onstage and play your banjo, and . . .

Before Sterling can finish his sentence, Butterbean is all over him like white on rice. It's a big commotion.

ANGLE—TABLE

Two big bouncers, EGGY and BORN KNOWLEDGE, fly into the fracas and separate the two combatants. Sterling is manhandled out of the club into the street. They pass two White men, MOE and JOSH FLATBUSH, brothers who co-own the club. Moe is the mouth. Josh is the numbers whiz.

CLOSE—MOE

MOE

This is a classy joint, a classy joint. I'm running a classy joint here.

CLOSE—JOSH

JOSH

Don't break nuthin'.

CLOSE—MOE

MOE

We ain't having it. This ain't uptown. This is "Beneath the Underdog."

CLOSE—JOSH

JOSH

A class operation.

ANGLE—RITA AND CORA

Rita and Cora are two of the waitresses at "Beneath the Underdog." They bounce from table to table, taking orders, taking tips, trying to make that money.

6   **INT:** *BLEEK'S LOFT—MORNING*

It's early morning and the CAMERA MOVES SLOWLY through Bleek's loft. There is hardly any furniture at all; however, WE DO NOTICE two big mural-size posters of Bleek's heroes in life—John Coltrane and Willie Mays. Finally WE COME UPON two figures underneath a giant red comforter. The alarm clock goes off.

CLOSE—ALARM CLOCK

ANGLE—BED

Bleek's head emerges from under the comforter and he drags himself out of bed and into the bathroom. The other body begins to stir also. Bleek comes back and sits on the bed.

BLEEK

Wake up! Wake up! Wake up!

Bleek pulls the comforter off the bed and WE SEE INDIGO still asleep, a very beautiful sister.

BLEEK

Ladybug! Let's go.

INDIGO

I don't want to go to school.

I don't want to go to school.

Bleek laughs because he realizes this is a reenactment of her childhood.

BLEEK

I'm not your father.

Ladybug gets up.

INDIGO

I'm up, was just dreaming.

BLEEK

Stop dreaming or you'll be late for school and all your students will have their little hearts broken.

INDIGO

Talkin' 'bout broken hearts, my moms always told me, don't ever marry a musician, let alone go out with one. You'll be inviting grief, tears, pain and heartbreak to your doorstep. She said, "Honey, let me tell you one thing. Leave those visitors outside. Don't let them into your home."

BLEEK

Your mother wasn't talking 'bout me.

INDIGO

Maybe not. Bleek, you're a good brother, but you still don't know what you want.

BLEEK

Now I guess it's time for Confessions of a Modern Day Dog.

INDIGO

Like it or not, Bleek, you're a *dog*. A nice dog, but a dog, nonetheless.

BLEEK

I won't argue the point. You know how I am. It's no secret. With men . . . It's a dick thing.

INDIGO

A dick thing?

BLEEK

A dick thing!

7   **EXT:** *BLEEK'S STOOP—MORNING*

As Bleek comes down his stoop he sees his father, Big Stop, already sitting there waiting. Big Stop used to be a minor league pitcher; he wears his old jersey and cap.

BIG STOP

Bleek, you're late.

BLEEK

Three minutes.

BIG STOP

Probably one of your lady friends no doubt held you up.

BLEEK

Not at all . . .

As if on cue, Indigo comes running out of the house.
CLOSE—BLEEK
He's busted.
ANGLE—INDIGO

INDIGO

Good morning, Mr. Gilliam; sorry I gotta run, late for school.
She kisses Big Stop on the cheek before she runs down the block.
ANGLE—STREET

BLEEK

How's the arm?

BIG STOP

I'm off the disabled list.

BLEEK

Good, let's throw.

This is their morning ritual, which is also the ritual of millions of other fathers and sons—playing catch. This is a large part of their communication. They start tossing the hardball back and forth.
CLOSE—BIG STOP

BIG STOP

You love her!
CLOSE—BLEEK

BLEEK

Like her.
CLOSE—BIG STOP

BIG STOP

What about the other one?
CLOSE—BLEEK

BLEEK

I'm not gonna lie. I love women and I find it hard to be with *just* one.
CLOSE—BIG STOP

BIG STOP

Just be careful of what you do ask for, you might get it.
CLOSE—BLEEK
He doesn't say anything.
CLOSE—BIG STOP

BIG STOP

And don't bring any babies into this world before you get married. If I see another sixteen-year-old, Black unwed mother pushing a stroller down the street, with another baby in the other arm, I don't know what I'll do.
CLOSE—BLEEK

BLEEK

I hear ya.
CLOSE—BIG STOP

BIG STOP

That's it. That's enough.
He feels his arm.
CLOSE—BLEEK

BLEEK

We just started.
ANGLE—STREET

BIG STOP

My arm feels funny.

BLEEK

Ya coming up?

BIG STOP

Naw. I'll go on home.

BLEEK

Call you later. Gotta take care of yourself.

BIG STOP

Just old, that's all.

Bleek hugs his father.

8   **INT:** *LOFT—MORNING*

Bleek is practicing his trumpet; first he's working on his scales . . .

DISSOLVE TO:

ANGLE—BLEEK

Bleek is still practicing, on to another segment of his daily program, working on his chords.

DISSOLVE TO:

CLOSE—BLEEK

Bleek works on his muted trumpet. Because of the different light we should be able to tell several hours have elapsed. Bleek is in full concentration when we hear the intercom buzzer. It buzzes several more times before he himself hears it.

ANGLE—BLEEK

Pissed, he goes to the intercom, presses a button, and a small TV screen comes on.

CLOSE—SCREEN

WE SEE a very attractive sister staring right INTO THE CAMERA. This is CLARKE, Bleek's other friend.

BLEEK (OS)

Clarke, what time is it?

She looks at her watch.

CLARKE

One o'clock.

CLOSE—BLEEK

BLEEK

And what does that mean?

CLOSE—SCREEN

CLARKE

You are practicing.

BLEEK (OS)

Right. I'm practicing, and if you know I'm practicing and you know I don't finish till two o'clock, which is for another sixty minutes, why are you buzzing my buzzer?

CLARKE

Because I love you.

ANGLE—BLEEK

He buzzes her in, leaves the door cracked open and walks into the kitchen.

ANGLE—KITCHEN

Bleek pours himself some water as Clarke kisses him.

BLEEK

How many times do I have to tell you I have a certain amount of hours allotted to practice daily? You know my program, yet you consistently overlook it.

CLARKE

I get the times mixed up. Everything with you is so damn regulated. A certain time to do this, a certain time to do that. Everything is on a schedule, a timetable. Loosen up, tight-ass.

BLEEK

Life is too short. I need it like this to do all the things I gotta do. I like order.

CLARKE

Order is fine, but your shit is ridiculous.

BLEEK

And what do you want?

CLARKE

When I think about what a man means to me, one of the first things that comes to mind is knowing what he wants, being decisive. You don't know what you want. Make up your mind. Be a *man*. Don't be wishy-washy on me.

BLEEK

I know what I want. My music! Everything else is secondary.

CLARKE

I knew you would say that.

BLEEK

Why'd you ask then?

CLARKE

Let me give you a tip. If your music is the be all to end all as you state, to ensure that, you better get rid of Giant as your manager.

BLEEK

Clarke, please stay out of my business. Thank you.

CLARKE

Are you fucking him, or what? He's a horrible manager. Everybody can see that but you.

BLEEK

Mind your damn business.

CLARKE

I'm looking out for your best interests.

BLEEK

Why are you bringing all this confusion into my home?

CLARKE

Bleek, I'm not saying I'm a very wise person, but everybody is a teacher. People can teach you two things. What to do or what not to do.

Bleek puts the trumpet in his mouth, looks at her while fingering the valves.

CLARKE

Say something.

BLEEK

Now that you have totally disrupted my program, we might as well make love.

Clarke laughs dead in his face.

CLARKE

Ha! For once let's be real. What you and I do is not make love.

BLEEK

What would you call it?

CLARKE

It's definitely not making love!

BLEEK

Boning!

CLARKE

You've been a lot more imaginative.

BLEEK

I got a million of them. *The Mo' Better.*

CLARKE

Mo' what?

BLEEK

The Mo' Better makes it Mo' Better.

CLARKE

Anyway, that's what we do. We don't make love, you don't love me.
But in the meantime I'll settle for some of that Mo' Better.

BLEEK

I also got some of that In Case of Emergency Break Glass Dick.

Clarke takes off her top and puts it on the end of his trumpet. Bleek follows her as
she leads him back to the bedroom.

8A   **INT:** *BLEEK'S BEDROOM—DAY*

Bleek continues to play his trumpet as Clarke disrobes and slides into the bed.

CLOSE—BLEEK

In SLOW MOTION Bleek removes the trumpet from his mouth but we still continue to hear his music in the BG.

JUMP CUT TO:

BLEEK

giving Clarke the "Mo' Better."

BLEEK (VO)

I don't know what you would call it, but whenever I'm making love to
a woman, I find myself thinking about another woman, about her
sexuality. Who knows, they might be thinking of some other guy too!

EXTREME CLOSE-UP—LIPS OF CLARKE AND BLEEK

Both are kissing passionately when Clarke gets caught up in the moment and bites
Bleek's lip by accident.

ANGLE—BLEEK AND CLARKE

Bleek jumps up like he's been shot.

BLEEK

Shit!

CLARKE

I'm sorry.

BLEEK

That's my fucking lip. Please don't *ever* do that again.

CLARKE

I was playing.

BLEEK

Don't play with my lips.

Bleek storms out of the bedroom into the bathroom.

CLOSE—CLARKE

She's visibly upset.

BLEEK (OS)

You cut my fucking lip, it's bleeding.

CLARKE

I'm sorry. Jesus Christ, I said I'm sorry.

BLEEK (OS)

You're nuts.

CLARKE

Let me kiss it to make it "mo' better."

She laughs.

BLEEK (OS)

Shit ain't funny.

CLARKE

I was joking . . . Alright, I won't kiss you ever again.

CLOSE—BLEEK

Bleek looks into the bathroom and inspects his lip.

BLEEK

Good. I make my living with my lips.

9   **INT:** *GIANT'S APARTMENT—DAY*

WE MOVE SLOWLY through the cluttered messy studio apartment. Stacks and stacks of old newspapers are everywhere; seated at the kitchen table is Giant with PETEY.

ANGLE—GIANT

Giant sits across the table from his bookie. The *New York Post* sports section is laid out in front of him.

GIANT

C'mon, Petey. I've been down before, but have I ever been out? Huh? Huh? No. I've never been out.

PETEY

Why don't you clean this place up. It's filthy.

GIANT

Cleanliness is next to Godliness.

PETEY

Down but never out? This is the last time I carry you.

Giant starts to circle his teams with a red pen.

CLOSE—PAPER

WE ARE TIGHT ON the *latest line* on today's baseball games.

CLOSE—PETEY

PETEY

Shoot!

GIANT

Finally. I'm putting down on all today's games.

PETEY

Shoot!

GIANT

Mets over Cards. Twins over Yanks. Dodgers, Pirates, Phils, Astros, Tribe, A's, Tigers. Red Sox, Blue Jays, and the Angels.

PETEY

All of that?

> **GIANT**
> All of that. Gimme two C-notes on each.

> **PETEY**
> Can you cover that?

> **GIANT**
> Just make the bet.

> **PETEY**
> Two C-notes on each game.

> **GIANT**
> I'll be back.

10   OMIT

11   **INT:** *"BENEATH THE UNDERDOG" CLUB—DAY*
Josh is behind the calculator, doing his numbers. He does not even look at the calculator, just the receipts and papers in front of him.

> **MOE**
> What does it look like?

> **JOSH**
> It looks good.

> **MOE**
> What do the numbers say?

> **JOSH**
> The numbers look good.

> **MOE**
> Good.

> **JOSH**
> The numbers never lie.

> **MOE**
> That's what I like about numbers. People start lying from the crib, but not numbers.

> **JOSH**
> Moe, the numbers never lie.

12   **EXT:** *"BENEATH THE UNDERDOG"—NIGHT*
People begin to line up early to get in.

13   **EXT:** *BACK ALLEY ENTRANCE—NIGHT*
Roberto stands outside the back alley entrance. This is where the musicians come into the club.
ANGLE—ALLEY—NIGHT
Bottom and Rhythm walk toward the door.

> **BOTTOM**
> Can the cat play?

> **RHYTHM**
> Is the day long?

> **BOTTOM**
> Very long!

> **RHYTHM**
> There you go. But he's so evil-looking he can kill a brick.

> **BOTTOM**
> That evil.

They stop as Roberto opens the door.

ANGLE—DOOR

ROBERTO

Good evening, Mr. Bottom. Mr. Rhythm.

BOTTOM

Roberto Clemente.

ROBERTO

Greatest ballplayer. Greatest.

14   **EXT:** *"BENEATH THE UNDERDOG"—NIGHT*

The line is even longer than before. What's interesting is the racial makeup of the
line. It's only half Black, the rest being young White middle-class and a flavoring
of Japanese couples.

ANGLE—LINE

Giant comes around the corner, stops and looks at the line.

CLOSE—GIANT

ANGLE—HIS POV

CLOSE—GIANT

WE TRACK with Giant as he walks past the line up to the entrance where Eggy
and Born Knowledge stand.

ANGLE—ENTRANCE

EGGY

No midgets allowed.

GIANT

The name is Giant.

BORN KNOWLEDGE

The circus left last week.

Giant ignores that crack.

GIANT

When are you gonna let the folks in?

EGGY

Lines are good for business.

GIANT

Is that you talking, or Moe and Josh?

BORN KNOWLEDGE

We can't have a smart thought? Why it got to be a White man? The
Black man is God.

GIANT

Born Knowledge, please don't start your five percenter shit, cuz I
don't want to hear it. Eggy, when are you letting people in?

EGGY

When it's time.

GIANT

And when is that?

BORN KNOWLEDGE

Time is when.

GIANT

The both of you can kiss my narrow black ass two times.

BORN KNOWLEDGE

Go in peace, my brother. Go in peace.

15   **INT:** *"BENEATH THE UNDERDOG"—NIGHT*

People begin to trickle in.

DISSOLVE TO:

MORE PEOPLE
taking their seats.

DISSOLVE TO:

THE CLUB
is almost full.

16 **INT:** *DRESSING ROOM—NIGHT*
The band is all there except Left Hand. Bleek is going over the numbers with the guys.

GIANT
Where's Left Hand?

SHADOW
Late again.

GIANT
Bleek?

BLEEK
I warned him.

RHYTHM
I talked to him earlier.

GIANT
Five will get you ten he's with Jeanne.

BOTTOM
That's a sucker's bet.

ANGLE—DOOR
Left Hand comes into the dressing room with his arm around a very attractive White woman, JEANNE.

LEFT HAND
Sorry I'm late.

JEANNE
We had trouble getting a cab.

GIANT
Left Hand, *you* are late.

JEANNE
We're sorry.
Bleek stares at Left Hand, but he just sits down with Jeanne.

LEFT HAND
What did I miss?

GIANT
If your late ass woulda been here you woulda missed nada.

BLEEK
We were going over the numbers.

LEFT HAND
Then I didn't miss anything.

CLOSE—GIANT
He tries to catch Left Hand's attention, as he motions for Jeanne to leave.
CLOSE—LEFT HAND
He's too busy messing with Jeanne to notice.
ANGLE—BLEEK

BLEEK
Jeanne, can you excuse us?

ANGLE—JEANNE AND LEFT HAND

LEFT HAND

Jeanne, get up.

CLOSE—GIANT

GIANT

All human beings who are not in this musical group please leave the dressing room.

CLOSE—JEANNE

She gets up too slow for Giant.

CLOSE—GIANT

GIANT

Let me repeat. If you ain't in this group, get the fuck outta here. *That means you!*

CLOSE—JEANNE

JEANNE

I'll be down front.

She leaves.

ANGLE—DRESSING ROOM

BLEEK

Left Hand, that's some *out* shit.

SHADOW

Bleek, let it go.

LEFT HAND

Why are y'all so hard on my lady?

GIANT

Your lady is fucking up, been fucking up. Y'know damn well nobody is allowed back here when we're about to go on. Everybody else's woman respects that shit except you and her.

LEFT HAND

It's because she's White.

GIANT

Because she's White?

LEFT HAND

You dog her out because she's White.

GIANT

Be real.

BLEEK

Be cool.

CLOSE—GIANT

GIANT

I have a brother just like you. When we were little he used to be an "Archie" comic book freak. If he had any money, that's where it went.

CLOSE—LEFT HAND

LEFT HAND

Is this a long story?

CLOSE—SHADOW

SHADOW

Shut up and listen.

CLOSE—GIANT

GIANT

Anyway, every issue they had these pinups of Betty and Veronica in bathing suits. My brother thought they were fine. One day he decided he was gonna put Betty and Veronica up all over our room. He tore out the pinups and Scotch-taped them to the wall.

CLOSE—BOTTOM

BOTTOM

And?

CLOSE—GIANT

GIANT

And my moms came into the room to check our homework. When she looked up and saw Betty and Veronica her eyes saw red. I said, "Get Larry, it wasn't me. I didn't do it. It was Larry's idea."

ANGLE—ROOM

The guys all laugh except Left Hand.

CLOSE—LEFT HAND

He's not amused.

CLOSE—GIANT

as he imitates his moms.

GIANT

If I ever—WHACK—see any White woman—WHACK—in my house again, I'LL KILL YOU—WHACK-WHACK. Do you understand me? WHACK.

CLOSE—BOTTOM

BOTTOM

And?

CLOSE—GIANT

GIANT

I started to cry. "Mommy, don't kill my only brother. Don't kill him. Don't kill him. He just loves Betty and Veronica."

CLOSE—LEFT HAND

LEFT HAND

And the moral of the story is?

CLOSE—GIANT

GIANT

There is no moral to the story. Just keep that bitch outta here.

LEFT HAND

Don't disrespect her like that. She's good to me. Show some respect.

GIANT

You show some respect.

ANGLE—DRESSING ROOM

BLEEK

Do it.

SHADOW

Pull her coattail.

BOTTOM

Do right, Left.

CUT TO:

16A **INT:** *"BENEATH THE UNDERDOG"—NIGHT*

ANGLE—TABLE
The people are carrying on.
CLOSE—BLEEK

BLEEK

Will the people at that table right there, yeah, youse people. Be quiet.
ANGLE—TABLE
They continue to talk *loud*.
CLOSE—BLEEK

BLEEK

Hey! Hey! Shut the fuck up. Show some respect, at least for the people who have paid their good money to *listen* and not run their damn mouth.
ANGLE—CLUB
The audience applauds.
CLOSE—BLEEK

BLEEK

We thank you for your time and consideration.
Bleek counts off the time and the band begins to play.
CLOSE—BLEEK'S MOUTH
In SLOW MOTION Bleek puts his trumpet into his mouth.

17   **INT: *"BENEATH THE UNDERDOG" OFFICE—NIGHT***
Giant knocks on the door and enters before Moe and Josh can answer. They are playing puff basketball in their suits.

GIANT

Did ya see the lines around the block?

MOE

We got eyes.

JOSH

We got ears.

GIANT

It's been like this consistently. Bleek's packing 'em in.
Josh looks at Giant.

MOE

We are pleased.

GIANT

Look, Moe and Josh, we're gonna have to get mo' money. You're making a killing. What's fair is fair.

MOE

What we're paying you now is *fair*. It's also what you agreed upon.

GIANT

C'mon, Moe.

MOE

It's out of the question.

GIANT

Everybody's making money except the artists.

MOE

Don't hand me that artist doo-doo. They don't have any financial risks . . . Go listen to the music.
He dismisses Giant with a wave of the hand.

GIANT

We'll get that money.

17A **INT:** *"BENEATH THE UNDERDOG" STAGE—NIGHT*
ANGLE—STAGE
The band finishes the song.
CLOSE—GIANT
He watches from the back and applauds.

18 **EXT:** *BROOKLYN BRIDGE—NIGHT*
Bleek is playing his horn on the walkway of the Brooklyn Bridge. It's a beautiful Manhattan skyline that listens to his horn. He nods to the occasional jogger who runs by.

19 **EXT:** *INDIGO'S APARTMENT—NIGHT*
Bleek is coming down the block when he sees Indigo, who is waiting for him.
ANGLE—STOOP
Bleek kisses her.

BLEEK

We had a great night. The cats were kickin' ass and takin' names; wish you coulda been there.

INDIGO

I'm glad it went well, but you know how I feel about clubs, all that smoke, it's not my thing. I'd rather sit home and listen to your records than be bothered by all those people.

Bleek is somewhat put off by this.

BLEEK

What are you saying?

INDIGO

You know I love your music, but I don't like sitting up in some smoky club. That's all.

BLEEK

Forget about it.

20 **INT:** *INDIGO'S APARTMENT—NIGHT*

BLEEK

Ya hungry?

INDIGO

It's too late to eat for me.

Bleek walks in a circle around Indigo who's lying down on the sofa.
CLOSE—INDIGO
She watches him.
CLOSE—BLEEK
He plays his trumpet as he circles her.
CLOSE—INDIGO

INDIGO

You say music is your everything. What would happen if you couldn't play any more? God forbid.

ANGLE—BLEEK
Bleek stops dead in his tracks.
CLOSE—BLEEK'S MOUTH
In SLOW MOTION he takes the trumpet out of his mouth.
ANGLE—BLEEK

> **BLEEK**
> I guess I would curl up in a corner and die.

ANGLE—INDIGO

> **INDIGO**
> In that case, let's get on our knees and pray right now.

They both laugh.

HIGH ANGLE

Bleek puts the trumpet back in his mouth and circles Indigo once again as she begins to nod to the soothing sound of his trumpet.

WE CRANE DOWN into a CLOSE UP of a sleeping Indigo. He wakes her up and they make LOVE.

FADE OUT.

FADE IN:

21   **INT:** *COFFEE SHOP—MORNING*

Giant sits at the counter and opens up the *New York Post* and turns directly to the baseball scores.

CLOSE—GIANT

He scans the scores.

> **GIANT**
> Fuck.

ANGLE—BOOTH

Petey sits behind him. He calls out:

> **PETEY**
> Giant, see the paper?

Giant turns around on his stool, then joins Petey.

> **GIANT**
> Yeah, I can read.

> **PETEY**
> Can you count? Cuz you owe. What are you gonna do?

> **GIANT**
> I can get the money.

> **PETEY**
> Ya way over as it is.

> **GIANT**
> And people in *hell* want *ice water*. Tell me something I don't know already.

> **PETEY**
> It's your dance.

> **GIANT**
> Gimme the *Mets, Twins, Reds, Pirates, Cubs, Astros, Tribe, A's, Red Sox, Blue Jays* and da *Angels.*

> **PETEY**
> The full schedule? How much?

> **GIANT**
> Five hundred on each.

> **PETEY**
> You're a big boy.

> **GIANT**
> That's what they say.

22   **EXT:** *BLEEK'S LOFT—MORNING*

Giant pushes the intercom.

CLOSE—GIANT

He looks up at the window, then pushes the intercom again.

> **BLEEK (VO)**
> Who?

> **GIANT**
> Giant.

Bleek buzzes him in.

23 **INT:** *LOFT—MORNING*

Bleek is in his pajamas with horn in hand.

> **GIANT**
> My main man.

> **BLEEK**
> No, you can't borrow any money.

> **GIANT**
> Hold up! Did I say anything 'bout borrowing some money? Did I?

> **BLEEK**
> I've known you since third grade.

> **GIANT**
> This is true, but that's not the nature of this visit, my brother.

> **BLEEK**
> Do you pray?

> **GIANT**
> Only when I need a winner. Like now.

> **BLEEK**
> That's messed up. I pray every morning.

> **GIANT**
> About what?

> **BLEEK**
> A lot of things.

> **GIANT**
> Like what?

> **BLEEK**
> For one thing, I ask God to deliver me daily from Anger, Lust, Ego, and Attachment.

> **GIANT**
> Three out of four ain't bad.

They both laugh.

> **GIANT**
> Let me add some gravity to the situation.

> **BLEEK**
> The word is levity.

> **GIANT**
> That too. I asked Moe and Josh for more money. They wouldn't budge. But I'm working on it.

> **BLEEK**
> While you're working on it, run this over to Shadow's crib.

He hands Giant a record album.

> **BLEEK**
> I borrowed it.

GIANT

He'll get it.

CUT TO:

24 **INT:** *SHADOW'S CONDO—DAY*
Shadow, unlike the rest of the band members, lives in Manhattan on the Upper West Side overlooking the Hudson River.

SHADOW

'Bout fucking time. Bleek borrowed this record a year ago.

GIANT

Hey!

SHADOW

It's out of print. This is an extremely rare out of print Bird. Tellya bitch not to ask me for nuthin if it takes a year to get it back.

GIANT

Look, I'm just a delivery man doing my job and I made the delivery. Tell ya beef to Bleek. I'm gonna space.

Giant follows Shadow into his bedroom.

25 **INT:** *BEDROOM—DAY*

SHADOW

Should I change the sheets?

GIANT

If they need changing.

SHADOW

I was blending this honey and my woman always bust me. Do you smell perfume?

GIANT

Shadow, you've lost your mind.

SHADOW

This is some serious shit. Do you smell perfume?

GIANT

No.

SHADOW

Smell the sheets.

Giant smells the sheets.

GIANT

Smells alright to me.

SHADOW

I don't know why I'm asking you anyway. She has a highly developed sense of smell, can sniff me out five miles away. No joke. Sometimes I think she must be part canine and shit. She also counts my rubbers.

GIANT

Naw.

SHADOW

I swear on my mother. She keeps an accurate count, was an accounting major in school. So I gotta go out and buy some more before she bust me again. One time I ran around the city a whole day trying to get a blue box of Trojans. She knows everything.

GIANT

Why go through all that?

SHADOW

Number one: I like her. Number two: She's a mother-fucker in bed.
Number three: She's got the body of life.

GIANT

Three good reasons.

SMASH CUT TO:

26   OMIT

27   **INT:** *BEDROOM—NIGHT*

Bleek and Clarke are in bed, having just finished a session of the "Mo' Better."

CLARKE

Roll over.

Bleek rolls on his stomach. Clarke begins to search, inspect his back for bumps to pop. She gets one.

BLEEK

Ouch.

CLARKE

Ooo! That was a good one.

BLEEK

That hurt.

CLARKE

Be still.

BLEEK

How's your voice lessons?

CLARKE

Good. I think I'm ready.

BLEEK

Ready! It takes years, not months.

CLARKE

Ready to accompany the band for a song at "The Dog."

Bleek doesn't say anything.

CLARKE

You think I'm not ready.

BLEEK

Just because we—see each other, that has nothing to do with the music. At best you're an OK singer with potential to be good. We can't, I can't compromise my shit.

Clarke is hurt, but it's the truth.

CLARKE

Thanks for nothing.

BLEEK

I don't mean to be cruel, but if we were married it would be the same deal.

Clarke finds another bump and *squeezes* the hell out of it.

BLEEK

Shit.

CLARKE

Look, nobody is asking you or anybody else for any handouts. Everyone needs a break. I thought you might be that person. Shoot me, I was wrong. I'm finished.

Bleek turns back over.

CLARKE

A lot of people say I'm a very good singer.

BLEEK

Good, go sing with them, not me.

CLARKE

Forget you. I still believe in myself.

BLEEK

You're supposed to.

CLARKE

Shadow says I can be a star.

BLEEK

He said that.

28   **INT:** *LOFT—NIGHT*

Bleek is sitting at the piano with just his boxer shorts on.

CLOSE—BLEEK

His eyes are closed.

ANGLE—BLEEK

He plays several chords. WE ARE WATCHING Bleek composing. He chooses to
do this on the piano instead of the trumpet.

CLOSE—BLEEK

He opens his eyes, takes the pencil from between his teeth and . . .

CLOSE—MUSIC PAPER

. . . writes the notes down.

ANGLE—BEDROOM DOOR

Clarke stands there with her Georgetown tank top on and WE DOLLY with her to
Bleek at the piano.

ANGLE—BLEEK AND CLARKE

She puts her hands on his neck and begins to massage it.

BLEEK

That feels very good, but please stop. I gotta get this idea down. It just
came in.

CLARKE

You never let me play.

BLEEK

Let me get this down first.

EXTREME CLOSE-UP—BLEEK'S EAR

Clarke puts her tongue in and around his ear.

CLARKE (OS)

Does it tickle?

BLEEK (OS)

Yes.

CLOSE—CLARKE

CLARKE

Let me leave the artist at work alone. The muse is visiting and Bleek
is truly inspired. Then he will share his newest, latest gift to the
world. Hallelujah.

As Clarke rambles on with her sarcastic speech, we fade down her sound, as Bleek
does the same.

CLOSE—BLEEK

He tunes her out.

BLEEK (VO)

The day you say to a woman, "I can't live without you" is the day she says, *"Prove it.* Prove it by loving only me. Don't love your work or anything else as much as me."

CLOSE—CLARKE

Her mouth is moving but we can't hear what she's saying. We hear instead:

BLEEK (VO)

No woman can respect you after you say there's nothing more to your life than what you have with her.

CLOSE—BLEEK

He's playing the piano.

CLOSE—CLARKE

We begin to fade up on her sound.

CLARKE

I'm outta here.

ANGLE—PIANO

Clarke leaves.

HIGH ANGLE—LOFT

Clarke goes back into the bedroom and slams the door while Bleek continues to write his song.

28A **EXT:** *STREET—MORNING*

We TRAVEL the length of a block as The Bleek Quintet minus Left Hand walks to their rehearsal. Giant carries Bleek's trumpet, bringing up the rear is Bottom pushing his bass which is on wheels. The Quintet is laughing loud, we see how despite several differences amongst the members everyone generally likes each other.

29 **INT:** *REHEARSAL SPACE—DAY*

The band is about to begin to rehearse. Everyone is there except Left Hand.

ANGLE—ROOM

Bleek hands out the parts; this is the song Bleek was composing in Scene 28.

BLEEK

This is something that came in last night.

ANGLE—BOTTOM

He holds his part out in front of him and reads the title.

BOTTOM

"Pop Top 40 R 'n' B Urban Contemporary Easy Listening Funk Love."

CLOSE—RHYTHM

RHYTHM

Bleek, you always come up with some *OUT* shit.

CLOSE—SHADOW

He stares at the music in front of him and he's not impressed.

SHADOW

Fuck this. Let's talk about the money.

GIANT

What about the money?

BLEEK

What about the money?

SHADOW

We want more.

GIANT

Are you the spokesperson for everyone?

SHADOW

Yeah.

GIANT

Even for Left Hand, who's late again?

SHADOW

Yep. We've been packing 'em in at "The Dog," Moe and Josh are making cash dollars. Where's our raise?

BOTTOM

You promised.

RHYTHM

Long overdue.

GIANT

I'm talking to them now.

BLEEK

He's working on it.

SHADOW

Maybe we need new management. Somebody who can get the terms we want.

GIANT

You be the manager then.

BLEEK

Shadow, you fail to realize this is my band. When you're running shit, then you can do what you want.

SHADOW

Won't be long from now.

BLEEK

Good, but until that majestical day happens, you do what the hell I say.

SHADOW

The midget should go.

ANGLE—DOOR

Left Hand rushes in.

LEFT HAND

Sorry I'm late.

BLEEK

And the same shit goes for you, Left Hand. You show up late one more time and your shit is over.

He hands him his part.

LEFT HAND

Sorry! I won't be late again.

GIANT

I know plenty of good piano players who want your gig.

CLOSE—BLEEK

BLEEK

Let's walk through this.

ANGLE—ROOM

The quintet begins to learn the parts to "Pop Top 40 R 'n' B Urban Contemporary Easy Listening Funk Love." Periodically they stop, ask questions, and Bleek answers how he wants it to be played.

Shadow continuously messes up and every time this happens Bleek stops him, makes the corrections, and they begin again.

CLOSE—BLEEK

He's listening intently, waiting for Shadow to fuck up.

CLOSE—SHADOW

Shadow plays.

CLOSE—BLEEK

Shadow fucks up.

BLEEK

Goddammit, Shadow. How many times do we gotta go over that bar? You got the motherfucking music in front of you. Are you blind? Read it.

CLOSE—SHADOW

SHADOW

This note feels better. I tried what you wrote, this sounds better to me.

He plays.

CLOSE—BLEEK

BLEEK

Tell you what, why don't you go outside, play what you want, all you want. We'll wait. Then when you're finished, come back and play what I wrote. Read the notes. It's my music! It's my band. Everybody got that?

CLOSE—RHYTHM

RHYTHM

Yeah.

CLOSE—BOTTOM

BOTTOM

Cool.

CLOSE—LEFT HAND

LEFT HAND

Uh huh.

CLOSE—BLEEK

BLEEK

Shadow.

CLOSE—SHADOW

SHADOW

It's your band, but I write songs, we all write. When are we gonna play some of our material?

BLEEK

We'll deal with that later.

SHADOW

We better.

LEFT HAND

Bleek, you're a dictator, not a leader.

CLOSE—BLEEK

BLEEK

If anybody don't like it, get your own band. From the top. A one. A two. A three.

ANGLE—ROOM

The quintet tries it again.

30 **INT:** *"BENEATH THE UNDERDOG"—NIGHT*

The band performs "Pop Top 40 R 'n' B Urban Contemporary Easy Listening Funk Love." Unlike the rehearsal, they are up on it, and it's a killer.

30A *BACKSTAGE—UNDERDOG—NIGHT*

Giant talks on his portable phone.

GIANT

Yeah. I can read.

PETEY (VO)

Giant, you're making me look bad. When I look bad, I don't like it.

GIANT

I'll get you your money.

PETEY (VO)

I don't care how you get it, just get it soon.

Petey hangs up.

GIANT

Petey. Don't hang up on me.

30B **INT:** *"BENEATH THE UNDERDOG" STAGE—NIGHT*

The group finishes the song, the members acknowledge the applause.

CLOSE—BLEEK

BLEEK

Shadow, that's the way to play it.

CLOSE—SHADOW

Shadow looks at him.

31 **INT:** *"BENEATH THE UNDERDOG" OFFICE—NIGHT*

Bleek stands in the middle of the office.

BLEEK

I'm not happy at all. When I'm not happy, I don't play good. When I don't play good, the music sounds like doo-doo. When the music sounds like doo-doo, nobody comes. We all lose money.

MOE

Bleek, you're a great talent, but you've got a lot of dead weight around your neck, dragging you down. That so-called manager of yours, Giant, that's a joke. He couldn't manage a little league team. When you're ready for some real management, then come see me. I gotta first cousin. He's top shelf. Handles only the best. Everything first-class, all the way. Just like me and Josh, first-class. Filet mignon.

JOSH

Dom Perignon. First-class.

BLEEK

I didn't come here to speak about Giant. I came here to speak about the great sums of money you two are making off my music and the little I see in return.

MO'
BETTER
SCRIPT

MOE

You are mistaken, cuz you're talking 'bout management. Giant, your *manager*, was the one who negotiated this deal. One you agreed to.

JOSH

And it's always been our business policy to never ever . . .

MOE

ever never . . .

JOSH

renegotiate the deal.

Bleek is stuck.

BLEEK

I've known him since third grade.

JOSH

That's not our concern.

MOE

Nobody's asking you not to be his friend. That's fine. We all need close friends.

JOSH

But *this is business*.

BLEEK

I trust him. He's honest. I can't say that about you, Moe, or your first-class cousin.

MOE

Nobody can be trusted. Everyone *steals*. Everyone is *crooked*. The trick is to walk out of the deal with as much of your shirt on as possible.

BLEEK

Y'know what that sounds like?

MOE AND JOSH

We like you.

BLEEK

Like the long, long history of Black artists being exploited.

MOE

Everybody exploits everybody.

BLEEK

I bet.

JOSH

It's about the green.

MOE

It's about da money.

CLOSE—BLEEK

He realizes he's dealing with two sharks.

CLOSE—MOE

MOE

In real life.

CLOSE—BLEEK

BLEEK

Giant is still my man.

CLOSE—MOE

MOE

Shoot yourself.

CLOSE—BLEEK

BLEEK

And my money?

CLOSE—JOSH

JOSH

We have a binding contract.

CLOSE—MOE

MOE

In real life,

31A **INT:** *UNDERDOG STAGE—NIGHT*

Butterbean is going through his act and the audience is dying.

ANGLE—GIANT

Giant stands at the bar laughing at Butterbean. The person standing next to him is smoking away.

GIANT

Hey, I'm allergic to smoke. Do me a solid.

The guy still continues to smoke.

Giant moves on and stops in his tracks.

ANGLE—CLUB

Giant sees Indigo and Clarke.

HIS POV

They both are entering the club at the same time. What's strange is that they're wearing the same dress; it only differs in color and size.

32 **INT:** *UNDERDOG DRESSING ROOM—NIGHT*

GIANT

Both Indigo and Clarke just walked in.

BLEEK

I got it.

GIANT

Bleek.

BLEEK

What?

GIANT

Ya owe me fiddy dollars. Remember that bet?

BLEEK

What bet?

GIANT

We were in Paris, I told you not to buy Indigo and Clarke the same shit.

BLEEK

Yeah, I remember.

GIANT

Do you remember us being in a rush, trying to make our plane, you said it was a million in one shot they would both wear it on the same day and see each other.

The realization is coming over Bleek's face.

BLEEK

Naw, it's a million in one.

GIANT

Wanna bet? Again!

BLEEK

Well, I'll be a motherfucker. Here. Good looking-out.
He peels off a fifty-dollar bill.

GIANT

That's what good managers do.

33 **INT:** *"BENEATH THE UNDERDOG" STAGE—NIGHT*
ANGLE—TABLE
Shadow pulls up a chair behind Clarke.

SHADOW

I don't know what you see in Bleek.
Clarke stares at him.

SHADOW

Alright. Alright, I admit he's a good cat and everything, but somebody
else, like me, could treat you the way you're supposed to be treated.
CLOSE—BLEEK
He surveys the club.
ANGLE—HIS POV—SLOW MOTION
He sees Shadow all over Clarke.
CLOSE—BLEEK
ANGLE—DIFFERENT POV—SLOW MOTION—MOVING POV
He also sees Indigo across the way and makes a beeline for her.
ANGLE—TABLE
Bleek pulls up a chair behind Indigo and kisses her.

BLEEK

What a pleasant surprise.

INDIGO

A big surprise.

BLEEK

How so?

INDIGO

You pissed in your pants when you saw me, especially since you
invited *Clarke*.

BLEEK

The surprise is seeing you here after you telling me how much you
hate clubs.

INDIGO

I had a sudden change of heart.

BLEEK

I'm happy you're here.

INDIGO

But is she happy? I like her dress!
Indigo points to Clarke.
ANGLE—CLARKE AND SHADOW
Shadow is pressing her.

SHADOW

I've heard you sing. I want to put you out in front, unlike Bleek. I'm getting my own shit. I'll be the boss. You'll be my vocalist.

CLOSE—CLARKE

All this time she hasn't said a word.

CLOSE—SHADOW

SHADOW

I understand you can't make that move now, it's chill. But remember what I said. All Bleek cares about is Bleek.

CLOSE—CLARKE

Shadow has hit a nerve. She responds.

CLARKE

Is that so?

SHADOW

So it is. Anything, anyone that might overshadow him, he blocks. Like myself. I should be the leader of this motherfucker, not Bleek. I'm getting my own shit.

CLOSE—CLARKE

She nods.

ANGLE—HER POV

Clarke spots Bleek sitting, talking to Indigo.

SHADOW (OS)

Clarke, I'd be the last person on earth to turn you against your man, but promise me you start to look and listen. You gotta let that love stuff go and look out for number one.

CLOSE—SHADOW

SHADOW

Promise?

CLOSE—CLARKE

CLARKE

Promise.

ANGLE—TABLE

Shadow gets up and leaves just as Bleek approaches them.

CLOSE—BLEEK

He looks at Shadow.

CLOSE—SHADOW—SLOW MOTION

He smiles back.

ANGLE—TABLE

Bleek sits down.

BLEEK

You should watch the company you keep.

CLARKE

I could say the same for you.

She motions toward Indigo who is staring right back.

BLEEK

Enjoy the set.

CLARKE

I like her dress.

34 **INT:** *"BENEATH THE UNDERDOG"—BACKSTAGE—NIGHT*
Bleek follows Shadow down the long corridor.

CLOSE—BLEEK

BLEEK

Shadow.

ANGLE—SHADOW

He stops.

CLOSE—BLEEK

BLEEK

Y'know, the last time I looked on Clarke's naked body, I didn't see my name, Bleek, on her. Not on her butt, her legs, her breast, nowhere. Nobody owns nobody.

CLOSE—SHADOW

SHADOW

You're absolutely right. Bleek, you should really listen to Clarke sing, or can you only hear your own music?

Shadow walks away.

ANGLE—BLEEK

Bleek is left standing with the bare truth burning in his ears.

35 **INT:** *BLEEK'S BEDROOM—NIGHT*

Bleek and Clarke this time are making love. This sequence will be a jumble, a COLLAGE of EXTREME, EXTREME CLOSE-UPS of parts of intertwined bodies. The intertwined parts are legs, arms, feet, toes, hands, and fingers.

CLOSE—BLEEK

He looks at Clarke.

ANGLE—HIS POV

Clarke stares at him.

CLOSE—BLEEK'S MOUTH

His mouth kisses her lips; when he finishes and moves away, WE SEE those lips belong to *Indigo*, not *Clarke*.

CLOSE—CLARKE

Clarke looks at Bleek.

The following sequence Bleek makes love to Indigo and Clarke at different times that is made up of a bunch of JUMP CUTS. In this flurry of CUTS, Indigo and Clarke become blurred, they become one and the same.

CLOSE—CLARKE

Smells his neck.

CLOSE—INDIGO

Smells his hair.

CLOSE—CLARKE

Begins to tickle his underarms.

CLOSE—BLEEK

BLEEK

Indigo, that tickles.

Oops. He fucked up.

CLOSE—CLARKE

CLARKE

Get off! What did you call me?

CLOSE—BLEEK

BLEEK

I called you your name.

CLOSE—CLARKE

CLARKE

The hell you did. I ain't deaf. Motherfucker, you called me Indigo.

CLOSE—INDIGO

INDIGO

Get off, Bleek, how in the hell could you call me her name? Here we
are, making love. I'm in your bed; Indigo, not Clarke.

CLOSE—CLARKE

CLARKE

I said Indigo, not Clarke.

CLOSE—INDIGO

INDIGO

I've had it. And you say you love me.

CLOSE—BLEEK

BLEEK

I never said that.

CLOSE—INDIGO

INDIGO

You did too.

CLOSE—BLEEK

BLEEK

Well, I don't remember it.

CLOSE—CLARKE

CLARKE

Do you remember saying you care?

CLOSE—BLEEK

BLEEK

Now *that* I remember.

CLOSE—CLARKE

CLARKE

If you say you care for me, why in the fuck are you still fucking
Indigo? Don't give me that "it's a dick thing" shit either.

CLOSE—BLEEK

What can he say?

CLOSE—INDIGO

INDIGO

Don't give me that "it's a dick thing" shit either.

CLOSE—BLEEK

He looks at the ceiling.

CLOSE—CLARKE

CLARKE

Why can't you look into my eyes? Why can't you? That's where the
true me is. Is it too real for you?

CUT TO:

CLOSE—INDIGO

INDIGO

You always avoid direct eye contact. Or is it something in you I might
see, the real you?

CUT TO:

CLOSE—CLARKE

**MO'
BETTER
SCRIPT**

CLARKE

Think about that?

CLOSE—BLEEK

He's struggling with something to say, something to explain himself. He has to do something because he's literally and figuratively being blasted from both sides.

CLOSE—BLEEK

BLEEK

The largest part of my heart is already taken, and if you can hang with that, fine. If not, let's not pretend. Let's not waste precious time. Life is too short.

CLOSE—CLARKE

She looks at Bleek.

CLARKE

Let's not pretend anymore.

CUT TO:

CLOSE—INDIGO

INDIGO

Life is too short.

CLOSE—BLEEK

He has nothing else to say. He picks up his trumpet and begins to play.

CLOSE—CLARKE

Clarke gets out of the bed.

CLOSE—BLEEK

He plays.

CLOSE—INDIGO

Indigo gets out of the bed.

36 **EXT:** *PROSPECT PARK—DAY*

Giant and Bleek are riding through the park doing laps on their ten-speed bikes.

37 **EXT:** *GAZEBO—DAY*

Bleek and Giant, both exhausted, sit down with the bikes under the gazebo which is on the lake.

BLEEK

Midget, you're doing a doo-doo job. You're fucking up. It's shit. Ca-ca.

GIANT

Why you wanna call me Midget? You OK'd the deal. You told me to get you into "The Dog" and I did. I got us the best terms we could get. The understanding was to get it on the back in, down the line.

BLEEK

This is down the line.

GIANT

And I'm working on it.

BLEEK

Not hard enough. Sometimes I think you're taking advantage of me.

Giant is hurt.

GIANT

How can you say that? That hurts to the quick. We grew up together. I'd rather chop off my left hand than take advantage of you. You're my boy. I'm your boy. You've saved my black ass on many a times.

BLEEK

Don't forget it.

GIANT

I'm breaking my fucking neck for you. Do I look like I'm getting rich offa you? There ain't no serious money in jazz, not *crazy, stupid* money. But I love you. I love the music. Somebody's been talkin' to you.

BLEEK

Nobody's talkin'.

GIANT

Bullshit. I gotta grapevine also.

BLEEK

All I'm saying is you gotta do a better job. It's about more than friendship.

GIANT

How many ass-whippings have you saved me from?

BLEEK

Too many to remember.

GIANT

You ain't lying.

BLEEK

One day I won't be around to save you. You're gonna have to take that ass-kicking.

GIANT

Let's break.
They get on their bikes.

GIANT

Can I get a loan?

BLEEK

Are you betting again?

GIANT

It's under control. What about the loan? Make it an advance.

BLEEK

How much?
Giant is hesitant to say the amount.

BLEEK

Whew! That much. Can't help you!
HIGH ANGLE—GAZEBO
Bleek and Giant ride off.
38   **EXT:** *STREET—DAY*
Bleek and Giant ride down the street and Giant turns the corner.
ANGLE—GIANT

GIANT

Later.
ANGLE—BLEEK
He waves.

BLEEK

Tonight.
ANGLE—STREET
Giant is speeding down the block when a parked car opens its door directly in front of him.
ANGLE—GIANT

He's airborne, flies up and over the car door and smashes into the street.
ANGLE—STREET
Two men, ROD and MADLOCK, drag a bloodied, dazed but conscious Giant into their car. They are laughing hysterically.
ANGLE—CAR
They speed away.

39 **INT:** *CAR—DAY*
The driver, Rod, remains silent as Madlock holds Giant up in the back seat.

MADLOCK
We're not gonna kill you. We don't believe in killing our brothers and sisters. But we gotta do something. It's only right.

He grabs Giant's left hand.
Madlock methodically breaks all of Giant's five fingers on his left hand. Even his screams can't drown out the snapping, the cracking of his bones. Once he's finished, he gives Giant his hand back.

MADLOCK
Are we gonna get our money?

GIANT
Yes.

MADLOCK
Yes only means something after you've said no.

GIANT
You'll get your money.

MADLOCK
We're gonna be nice and drop you off at Brooklyn Hospital, get your hand fixed.

40 **INT:** *CLASSROOM—DAY*
Indigo is in front of her third-grade class, teaching. It's an inner-city school, so you know all the kids are Black or Puerto Rican.
ANGLE—INDIGO

INDIGO
Who likes music?

ANGLE—CLASS
They all respond, "I do, I do," and raise their hands.
CLOSE—INDIGO

INDIGO
Where does music come from?

CLOSE—SHANIKA

SHANIKA
Music comes from people.

CLOSE—INDIGO

INDIGO
Good answer, Shanika. Let me make the question clearer. How is music made?

CLOSE—BENNY

BENNY
From instruments, Miss Downes.

ANGLE—INDIGO

INDIGO

That's right. Today I brought in some instruments. As I hold them up,
I want you to call out the name. You don't have to raise your hand.

She holds up a violin.

CLASS (OS)

Violin.

She holds up a flute.

ANGLE—CLASS

CLASS

Flute.

DIFFERENT ANGLE—CLASS

CLASS

Guitar.

CLOSE—INDIGO

INDIGO

This is my favorite musical instrument.

Indigo holds up a trumpet.

CLOSE—SHANIKA

SHANIKA

Trumpet.

SMASH CUT TO:

40A   **INT:** *BLEEK'S LOFT—DAY*

CLOSE—BLEEK

Bleek is blowing away, a man and his horn.

CUT TO:

41   **INT:** *REHEARSAL SPACE—DAY*

Clarke is taking her voice lessons from a rotund Black woman, MRS. PEARL.

CLOSE—MRS. PEARL

She sits at the upright piano and instructs Clarke.

MRS. PEARL

The voice is also an instrument, yes it is. And it should be treated as
such.

ANGLE—CLARKE

Clarke does her voice exercises. *She can really sing.*

42   **INT:** *CLASSROOM—DAY*

ANGLE—INDIGO

INDIGO

Class, let's sing the song Mr. Bleek Gilliam wrote for you.

ANGLE—CLASS

The class sings.

CUT TO:

43   **INT:** *BLEEK'S LOFT—DAY*

The children's singing continues as Bleek plays along with them.

CUT TO:

44   **INT:** *REHEARSAL SPACE—DAY*

The sound of the children singing and Bleek playing continues as Clarke comes in
with voice exercises which fit in perfectly.

CUT TO:

45   **INT:** *CLASSROOM—DAY*

The class sings.

46 **INT:** *BLEEK'S LOFT—DAY*
Bleek plays.

47 **INT:** *REHEARSAL SPACE—DAY*
Clarke ends the song.
CLOSE—MRS. PEARL

MRS. PEARL

Very good.

48 **INT:** *BLEEK'S LOFT—NIGHT*
Big Stop, who's a great cook, is preparing a big feast for the band, their dates, and an assortment of Bleek's friends, colleagues, and fellow artists.
ANGLE—KITCHEN
Big Stop is busy at work, kicking people who are "starvin' like Marvin" out of the kitchen.

BIG STOP

Get out of the kitchen. Don't mess with me while I'm working. Food
will be ready soon enough.
ANGLE—DOOR
Giant walks in with his left hand in a huge cast. Everyone gathers around him.

RITA

Poor baby, what happened?

GIANT

Fell off my bike.

BLEEK

When did that happen?

GIANT

Right after I left you.

BLEEK

That's a drag.

CORA

You gonna be alright?

GIANT

Good as new.
A crowd is still around Giant as they further inquire about the injury. Giant is all of a sudden beginning to like all of the attention.
ANGLE—SHADOW
He watches this in amusement.
ANGLE—HIS POV—SLOW MOTION
People all over Giant.
CLOSE—SHADOW

SHADOW

Hey, Midget. I told you 'bout sticking your hand in the cookie jar.
CLOSE—GIANT

GIANT

Actually, ya moms got *raw* and crossed her thighs too quick.
ANGLE—PEOPLE

PEOPLE

Oooo!
CLOSE—GIANT

MO'
BETTER
BLUES

He laughs.
CLOSE—SHADOW

SHADOW

Alright, ya gonna need another cast, keep fucking around.
CLOSE—GIANT

GIANT

You started it.
CLOSE—BLEEK

BLEEK

Take that outside.
ANGLE—KITCHEN

BIG STOP

Food's ready.
The confrontation is quickly forgotten about, folks is *hungry* and they line up to be served.
ANGLE—BLEEK AND GIANT

BLEEK

I don't believe your story.

GIANT

I hit a pothole.

BLEEK

Still don't believe it.
ANGLE—CORNER
Rhythm and Bottom sit in a corner devouring Big Stop's giant shrimp Creole gumbo. The following exchange should be done in the style of the old Black minstrel acts. *NOTE:* This should play as a TWO SHOT. NO CUTTING.

RHYTHM

Y'know my lady Lucindy?

BOTTOM

The one with the big . . .

RHYTHM

Not her, the one with the little . . .

BOTTOM

Oh, her.

RHYTHM

Tomorrow is her birthday and I want to get her something really nice.
Like a . . .

BOTTOM

No, not that. How about a . . .

RHYTHM

She hates them.

BOTTOM

Too bad. How 'bout a dress?

RHYTHM

My man. One of those sexy little foxy . . .

BOTTOM

Naw, too tight. Get her one of those loose . . .

RHYTHM

Too big. The in-between one, not too tight, not too loose.

BOTTOM

That'll work. I just bought one myself for . . .

RHYTHM

Thought you got rid . . .

BOTTOM

That was Vicky, her best friend. Dress will cost you around . . .

RHYTHM

That's too much money. I can't afford it. I got to get a dress that costs
no more than . . .

BOTTOM

Can't get it that cheap.

RHYTHM

I'll buy her a less expensive dress, also take her out to dinner.

BOTTOM

Good idea. We should go out together, a double date.

RHYTHM

Bet. But I heard ya girl is a wild . . .

BOTTOM

That's her second cousin, who's married to Lil' Love.

RHYTHM

Oh. Because on our first date we did the . . .

BOTTOM

No, you didn't.

RHYTHM

Yes, we did.

BOTTOM

I heard different. Thought that was . . .

RHYTHM

Not that time.

BOTTOM

So when are you coming to pick us up?

RHYTHM

Around . . .

BOTTOM

Too early . . .

RHYTHM

Then what about . . .

BOTTOM

Too late. Maybe around . . .

RHYTHM

Perfect.

BOTTOM

That's what I like about you and me. We complement each other like
the drum and the bass.

ANGLE—BLEEK

Bleek is holding court.

BLEEK

I'm convinced Black folks are ignorant. We just plain are. I'm sick
and tired of playing before everybody but my own people. They don't
come out. We don't support our own. If Black artists, if I had to rely

on niggers to eat, I'd starve to death. Jazz is our music, but we don't support it. It's sad, but true.

                              SHADOW
Bleek, you're fulla shit. People like what they like. If grandiose motherfuckers like you presented the music in a way that they like it, motherfuckers would come.

                              BLEEK
Oh yeah!

                              SHADOW
Yeah! That's the way I'm gonna do it. Black folks will come. You watch.

ANGLE—LEFT HAND AND JEANNE
Left Hand and Jeanne are eating together, enjoying themselves.

                              JEANNE
Honey, will you get me a glass of wine. Thank you.
Left Hand gets up.

                                                    JUMP CUT TO:

SAME ANGLE
                              JEANNE
Honey, will you get me a napkin, please.
Left Hand gets up.

                                                    JUMP CUT TO:

SAME ANGLE
                              JEANNE
Honey, will you get another fork. This one just dropped.
Left Hand gets up.

                                                    JUMP CUT TO:

ANGLE—GIANT AND SHADOW
                              GIANT
Shadow . . .

                              SHADOW
I'm busted.

                                                    JUMP CUT TO:

ANGLE—GIANT AND BOTTOM
                              BOTTOM
Ya already owe me three hundred bucks.

                                                    JUMP CUT TO:

ANGLE—GIANT AND RHYTHM
                              RHYTHM
No!

                                                    JUMP CUT TO:

ANGLE—GIANT, JEANNE AND LEFT HAND
                              GIANT
I need this solid. I wouldn't be asking if I didn't need it.
                            LEFT HAND
I need to get this back.
Left Hand takes out his wallet and peels off five hundred-dollar bills.
                              GIANT
Thanks a lot.

JEANNE

I don't appreciate you calling me a White bitch.
CLOSE—GIANT

GIANT

Jeanne, all I can do is apologize. I'm sorry, it won't happen again.
ANGLE—BUTTERBEAN, RITA AND CORA
Butterbean, who has had a few drinks, is getting loose and openly flirts with Rita and Cora.
ANGLE—BIG STOP
Big Stop is rapping hard to a very pretty woman who is at least fifty years his junior.
Bleek interrupts him.

BLEEK

Daddy, let me show you something? Excuse us.
Bleek leads his father back into the kitchen.
ANGLE—KITCHEN

BLEEK

You are seventy-five years old. Daddy, you've earned the right to do whatever you please, but leave the teenagers alone.

BIG STOP

Is she that young?

BLEEK

Yes. She would probably give you a massive coronary.

BIG STOP

Doubt it. You better pray you can do what I can at my young age.
JUMP CUT TO:

49   **EXT:** *BLEEK'S LOFT—MORNING*
Bleek and Big Stop are having their morning ritual of catch.
CLOSE—BLEEK

BLEEK

What can you do? You're seventy-five years old.
CLOSE—BIG STOP

BIG STOP

Don't ever bet against me. I'm still ya father and I'm still *healthy*.
Who taught you everything you know?
CLOSE—BLEEK

BLEEK

You did.
CLOSE—BIG STOP

BIG STOP

Alright then. Who taught you how to satisfy a woman?
CLOSE—BLEEK

BLEEK

You did.
CLOSE—BIG STOP

BIG STOP

How to always hold a little something back so they'll always come back for more.
CLOSE—BLEEK

BLEEK

Daddy, it was you.

CLOSE—BIG STOP

BIG STOP

Goddamn right it was me. Who taught you to gently suck a soft, sweet, luscious, juicy, tender nipple like a newborn baby being breast-fed for the very first time by his loving mother?

CLOSE—BLEEK

BLEEK

I learned that myself.

CLOSE—BIG STOP

BIG STOP

The hell you did. It was I. I'm ya daddy. *Big Stop Gilliam.* I brought ya rusty, crusty black ass into this world, along with your mother, God bless her soul. We gave you your life, your seed. Boy, the night you were conceived your mother jumped my bones after the game.

CLOSE—BLEEK

He stops his throw.

CLOSE—BIG STOP

BIG STOP

Boy, you were conceived in a segregated Pullman sleeping car. Somewhere on the tracks between St. Louis and Chicago.

CLOSE—BLEEK

He walks toward his father.

BLEEK

You never told me that.

ANGLE—BLEEK AND BIG STOP

BIG STOP

You never asked. You got to remember to always ask the *right question*.

BLEEK

Daddy, will there ever be a time when I'm your equal and not just your son?

BIG STOP

No.

They both laugh.

50 **EXT:** *STREET—DAY*

Giant is walking down the street; he's cautious. He quickly turns around to see anybody walking up behind him.

51 **EXT:** *GIANT'S APARTMENT BUILDING—DAY*

As Giant turns the corner, he sees a car parked across the street from his building. It's not Madlock and Rod in it, but two more HOODS, COOLEY and SMITH. Giant slowly makes an about-face.

CLOSE—GIANT

WE ARE CLOSE ON Giant's grim face as WE DOLLY with him down the block. His shit looks bleak.

51A **INT:** *TOWER RECORDS—JAZZ SECTION*

CLOSE—HANDS

A pair of hands go through the many CD's of John Coltrane, each different one is pulled out of the stack.

ANGLE—CASHIER

Shadow slams a pile of the Coltrane CD's on the counter.

CLOSE—CLARKE

Clarke stands behind the cash register, this is her gig until she gets that shot.

CLARKE

Hi, Shadow. How you doing?

CLOSE—SHADOW

SHADOW

Fine. Like yourself.

She plays it off.

ANGLE—CLARKE AND SHADOW

CLARKE

Will this be cash or charge?

SHADOW

Charge. Do you accept the Gold American Express card here?

CLARKE

Yes, we do.

SHADOW

Been a card member since 1989.

Clarke takes his card, puts it through the check. While she rings up his CD's, Shadow is rappin' hard, trying all his best lines.

CLOSE—CLARKE

CLARKE

I'm sorry, Shadow, but there is a security check on your card, and I will have to confiscate it.

CLOSE—SHADOW

SHADOW

Hold up. There's gotta be a mistake. I just paid that mother. Call 'em back.

CLOSE—CLARKE

CLARKE

You can look right here.

ANGLE—CLARKE AND SHADOW

He leans over the counter and looks at the credit card computer.

SHADOW

I got those CD's anyway.

CLARKE

Why are you here?

SHADOW

I wanted to see ya.

Clarke takes the CD's off the counter.

SHADOW

Ho! Ho! Leave this one out. I got cash. I'm gonna buy this one for you. Check it out. LOVE BALLADS.

52 **INT:** *"BENEATH THE UNDERDOG"—NIGHT*

The quintet is on stage, and Bleek moves to the microphone.

CLOSE—BLEEK

BLEEK

No matter what you do in music, sooner or later, eventually you're gonna come back to the blues.

ANGLE—STAGE
The band begins to play underneath Bleek.
CLOSE—BLEEK

We all know what the blues is? Right?
ANGLE—AUDIENCE

AUDIENCE

Right.
CLOSE—BLEEK

BLEEK

I thought so. I knew you knew. This is the "Both of My Women Done
Left Me" blues.
ANGLE—AUDIENCE
They laugh.
CLOSE—BLEEK

BLEEK

The "Double Blues."
ANGLE—STAGE
Bleek joins the band with his muted trumpet. The music continues as WE FLASH-
BACK TO:

53   **EXT:** *BLEEK'S ROOF—NIGHT*
It is a cool fall night and Bleek and Indigo are huddled up under a blanket.

BLEEK

Can you remember how you felt the first time you fell in love? Can
you?

INDIGO

September 25, 1980. My senior year in high school. A tall, fine Black
specimen, Vance Collins . . .

BLEEK

Alright! Alright. Didn't know what hit me. Bleek was the *original* fool
in love. That shit was so pure, so innocent. She felt the same way too.

INDIGO

How recent was this?

BLEEK

In third grade.

INDIGO

Third grade! And I was worried.

BLEEK

One day after passing notes back and forth all week, we met at three
o'clock in the schoolyard and kissed. When her lips touched mine I
flew straight to heaven, never felt like that since.

INDIGO

Not even with me?

BLEEK

I'm not gonna lie. Ever since then I've been trying to regain that
feeling.
Indigo gets out from under the blanket.

INDIGO

What are you saying?

MO'
BETTER
SCRIPT

BLEEK

I'm telling you something about me. All I hear from you is how I never communicate, don't open up to you.

INDIGO

Haven't you ever been close to the feeling?

BLEEK

With a woman?

INDIGO

No, with an elephant.

BLEEK

Only when I play my music.

INDIGO

I'm leaving.

BLEEK

Indigo.

INDIGO

Here we are, supposed to be lovers. I'm your woman and you tell me straight to my face you've never been in love since you kissed some ponytail, knock-kneed, skinny-leg girl in second grade.

BLEEK

Third grade.

INDIGO

Whatever, and I'm supposed not to be the least bit upset. No, I'm not upset. *I'm fucking furious.*

BLEEK

Why you gotta curse?

INDIGO

I'll curse up a motherfucking blue streak if my heart so desires. Motherfucker—Shit—Bastard—Cocksucker—Asshole . . .

Indigo stops as she realizes how foolish she sounds. She's not really good with profanity. She laughs.

INDIGO

Why don't you try and find that third-grade girl, marry her and live happily ever after.

Bleek stands up, walks to Indigo and puts the blanket around the both of them.
CLOSE—BLEEK AND INDIGO

INDIGO

Bleek, I'm not with this.

CUT TO:

54   **INT:** *"BENEATH THE UNDERDOG"—NIGHT*
ANGLE—STAGE
The band finishes the song.
ANGLE—AUDIENCE
They applaud.
CLOSE—BLEEK

BLEEK

The blues.
He takes a bow.
ANGLE—GIANT
Giant is standing in the back, watching, when Eggy approaches him.

EGGY

Moe and Josh want to see ya now.

55   **INT:** *"BENEATH THE UNDERDOG"—OFFICE*

MOE

How's the hand?

JOSH

If you need a good doctor I got a hand specialist.

Giant nods.

MOE

Good health is everything.

JOSH

You got good health you got everything.

MOE

This is a small world and people talk.

JOSH

We know of your problem.

MOE

You need help?

JOSH

We can help.

GIANT

And out of the goodness of your heart you want to help me?

MOE

God helps those who helps themselves.

JOSH

We're honest businessmen.

MOE

We like to make you an offer.

GIANT

I got two things to say: We still want more money and I'm still Bleek's manager.

MOE

I'm sorry to hear both things.

GIANT

They might as well break both my legs cuz I don't think I can come up with that much.

JOSH

We could.

MOE

That's the tragedy.

JOSH

What doesn't come out in the wash comes out in the rinse.

MOE

Shit shakes out.

Giant turns around and feigns a big limp as he leaves the office.

CLOSE—MOE AND JOSH

JOSH

He's going down quick.

56   **EXT:** *BACK ALLEY—STAGE DOOR—NIGHT*

Bleek says good night to Roberto and walks down the long, dark alley when Giant emerges from the shadows.

GIANT

Bleek.

BLEEK

Damn, you scared me.

GIANT

I need a place to stay.

BLEEK

For tonight?

GIANT

For a while.

BLEEK

C'mon.

GIANT

My brother.

57   **INT:** *BLEEK'S LOFT—NIGHT*

GIANT

I talked to Moe and Josh again.

BLEEK

What happened?

GIANT

The contract. We're stuck.

BLEEK

It's time to get a real lawyer.

GIANT

I got one.

BLEEK

Who?

GIANT

My brother-in-law.

BLEEK

Your brother-in-law Moses? Hell no.

GIANT

He's cheap.

BLEEK

Fuck dat. I'm fuckin' sick and tired of your fuckin' relatives. Your cousin the accountant, your uncle the plumber, your niece the dentist, my mouth is still fucked up behind that shit. I hate to tell you, but ya gotta fucked-up family.

GIANT

Hey, c'mon, Bleek.

BLEEK

I'm through with your relatives.

GIANT

They love you, always supported you.

BLEEK

Don't care.

GIANT

Alright, already. I'm here to do your bidding. That's my job.

Bleek picks up his trumpet and begins to finger it.

CLOSE—BLEEK

BLEEK

How much do you owe?

Giant doesn't want to say.

CLOSE—GIANT

GIANT

I'm afraid to say.

CLOSE—BLEEK

BLEEK

Write it down then.

He slides Giant a piece of paper.

ANGLE—BLEEK AND GIANT

Giant takes the pen and writes down the figure and slides it back to Bleek. Bleek falls back onto the sofa after reading it.

BLEEK

Ain't that a bitch. That much?

GIANT

Hit a bad-luck streak.

BLEEK

Look, Giant, I'm gonna see how much I can raise, but you gotta get help, that means your gig is over. I've been contemplating about managing myself. I have to be in control.

Giant's face is frozen.

GIANT

Is that what you want?

BLEEK

That's what I want.

GIANT

You're cutting everybody off; me, Indigo, Clarke.

BLEEK

I'm not cutting off nobody. Just doing what's best for me. Besides, Indigo and Clarke left me.

GIANT

That ain't what I heard. Bleek, how long have we been friends?

BLEEK

Since third grade.

GIANT

Doesn't that count for anything?

BLEEK

It has! You would have been long gone before now.

GIANT

You've been that displeased?

BLEEK

Doesn't matter. Anyway, the offer still stands. You can stay here and I'll try and get you that money before you get yourself killed, but you gotta do something about that damn gambling.

GIANT

I know, Bleek. I'm sick. I'm sick.

DISSOLVE TO:

58   **INT:** *BLEEK'S LOFT—NIGHT*

Giant is fast asleep on the sofa and WE DOLLY INTO Bleek's bedroom where he is dialing a number.

BLEEK

Hello.

INDIGO (VO)

Peace. I'm unable to come to the phone right now. Please leave a message after the tone.

CUT TO:

59   **INT:** *INDIGO'S BEDROOM—NIGHT*

Indigo is preparing her lessons for tomorrow's class. She looks at the answering machine.

BLEEK (VO)

Indigo, this is me. Calling to see how you are doing. I miss you. Call me if and when you feel like it. Later.

CLOSE—INDIGO'S FACE

CUT TO:

60   **INT:** *BLEEK'S BEDROOM—NIGHT*
CLOSE—BLEEK

BLEEK

Clarke, this is Bleek. What's up?

CUT TO:

61   **INT:** *CLARKE'S BEDROOM—NIGHT*
CLOSE—SOPRANO SAXOPHONE

The CAMERA SLOWLY MOVES from the sax to clothes thrown on the floor to Clarke and Shadow in the bed making love ferociously.

BLEEK (VO)

Shadow says you're coming along great. Maybe I was wrong, you can sing.

Clarke tries to reach for the answering machine to turn it down, but Shadow grabs her hand.

CLARKE	BLEEK (VO)
Let me turn it down.	Haven't seen or heard from you
SHADOW	in a while. You should come
Naw, I want ya to hear this.	down to the club. I was just
	checkin' in. Call me.

ANGLE—SHADOW AND CLARKE

SHADOW

He's begging. I want to make ya a full-time gig.

CLARKE

What about the rest?

SHADOW

Gone. See ya. I'm trying to build something with you. I swear on my mother's grave, so help me God.

CLARKE

I don't believe anything a man says.

SHADOW

In this case, believe me. The rest of the time you should believe only half of what men say. Half is truth, half is bullshit.

CLARKE

Which half are you?

SHADOW

Half.

CLARKE

Half of what?

SHADOW

Half.

CLARKE

See! I don't believe anything a man says.

CUT TO:

62 **INT:** *BLEEK'S BEDROOM*
ANGLE—BLEEK
He hangs up the phone.
CLOSE—BLEEK
In SLOW MOTION Bleek puts the trumpet in his mouth.

SMASH CUT TO:

63 **EXT:** *BROOKLYN BRIDGE—NIGHT*
WE ARE TIGHT ON Bleek's mouth, then CRANE UP TO SEE a solitary figure practicing his trumpet and we

FADE OUT.

FADE IN:

64 **EXT:** *BLEEK'S LOFT—MORNING*
Bleek and Big Stop are playing catch.
CLOSE—BIG STOP

BIG STOP

So you finally got the sense to ask your daddy about some of all this knowledge I got.
CLOSE—BLEEK

BLEEK

Just answer the question.
CLOSE—BIG STOP

BIG STOP

You can't rush the knowledge. You wanna know which woman is for real.
CLOSE—BLEEK

BLEEK

Daddy!
CLOSE—BIG STOP

BIG STOP

When a person gets to a certain level of accomplishment and people come into their life, you don't know whether it's because of their position, possessions or reputation, whatnot, or whether it's cuz of your character.
CLOSE—BLEEK

BLEEK

You saying it's character.

MO'
BETTER
SCRIPT

CLOSE—BIG STOP

BIG STOP

Character, a sweet and understanding heart. That's what I judge
people by.

CLOSE—BLEEK

BLEEK

Then what?

CLOSE—BIG STOP

BIG STOP

Right! It's not that easy. Some people are real good at hiding, not
revealing their true nature, what they're really 'bout. A lot of times the
only way you find out is if a crisis arrives.

CLOSE—BLEEK

BLEEK

Are you saying I have to be in a car accident to know?

CLOSE—BIG STOP

BIG STOP

Son, I hope not, but it be's like that sometime.

65 **INT:** *"BENEATH THE UNDERDOG"—NIGHT*
ANGLE—STAGE

Butterbean is doing his rendition of a Mississippi Wayback Bayou Blues number.

66 **INT:** *DRESSING ROOM—NIGHT*

A barber who the cats call CHERRY is hooking up their heads. We hear the kind
of talk one hears in the neighborhood barbershop.

67 **EXT:** *BACK ALLEY—STAGE DOOR—NIGHT*

Giant is waiting at the backstage entrance when Bleek approaches.

GIANT

Yo, you got the money yet?

BLEEK

I'm working on it.

GIANT

Don't work *too* long.

BLEEK .

In the meantime, stay out of the spotlight . . . So what are you gonna
do?

Giant pauses, then . . .

GIANT

In the immortal words of Darryl Dawkins, "When all is said and done,
there's nothing left to say or do."

BLEEK

Whatever happened to him?

GIANT

I don't want to start any trouble, y'know me. I like peace.

BLEEK

Get to the point.

GIANT

I'm not your manager no mo', but you're still my boy. I got your best
interest at heart. Even though you and Clarke ain't hanging yet . . .

BLEEK

C'mon.

GIANT

Shadow is boning Clarke.

CLOSE—BLEEK

His face is frozen.

FLASH CUT TO:

67A   **INT:** *CLARKE'S APARTMENT/BEDROOM—NIGHT*
CLOSE—SHADOW AND CLARKE

They are boning.

67B   **EXT:** *BACK ALLEY—STAGEDOOR—NIGHT*
CLOSE—BLEEK

BLEEK

Ya sure?

CLOSE—GIANT

GIANT

Wanna bet?

CLOSE—BLEEK

BLEEK

Fuck it. I hope they're happy. Ya positive?

CLOSE—GIANT

GIANT

Bleek, wake up and smell the decaf.

Bleek shakes his head, Giant follows him into the club as Roberto holds the stage
door open.

68   **INT:** *BACKSTAGE*

Shadow walks up to Bleek.

SHADOW

Me and the other cats want to have a meeting with you after the set.

BLEEK

Shadow, get out of my face.

SHADOW

We wanna talk.

Bleek pushes Shadow away.

BLEEK

I said get outta my face.

Giant rushes in between them, before they come to blows, like a referee instructing
two boxers before a championship bout.

GIANT

Alright. Let's have a fair fight. Bare skin. NO PUNCHES IN THE
MOUTH. Fuck 'em up, Bleek.

SHADOW

I'm gonna kick ya "Both My Two Women Done Left Me Double
Blues"-ass . . .

Before Shadow can say another word, Bleek clips him on the side of the head. The
members of the band cheer both men on.

GIANT

Bing. Upside the head. Do the Tyson. Do the Tyson.

Shadow charges Bleek and knocks him down and they roll around on the floor.
Eggy and Born Knowledge come flying into the fracas and try to pry them apart.

BORN KNOWLEDGE

Stop this madness now. Ya acting just like the White man wants us to act.

EGGY

You gotta show to do. Let's go.

GIANT

Let 'em work it out. Work it out.

The combatants are separated; Eggy has Bleek and Born Knowledge has Shadow.

BLEEK

You're fired.

SHADOW

Fuck you, I quit. I'm getting my own shit.

BLEEK

Fired! Quit! See ya!

SHADOW

You're a punk.

BLEEK

Any of you cats who wants to follow your ringleader, go with him here now.

Nobody moves; they are not stupid, they have bills to be paid. This is a steady gig.

SHADOW

Anyway, ya never loved her.

69   **INT:** *"BENEATH THE UNDERDOG"—NIGHT*
ANGLE—MEN'S ROOM—NIGHT
Giant comes into the men's room and up to a urinal.
ANGLE—BATHROOM STALLS
Rod and Madlock emerge from two adjoining stalls and surprise Giant who has just zipped up his pants.
ANGLE—MEN'S ROOM

MADLOCK

We don't believe in killing our brothers and sisters, but you're definitely gonna be *hurt.*

CLOSE—GIANT
A realization comes over his face. He's done. This is going to be one serious ass-kicking and nobody, not even Bleek, can get him outta this one.

GIANT

And I think that's about it, sports fans. The game is over, the fat lady has sung. I can hang it up. It's ovah. O-V-A-H.

69A   **INT:** *"BENEATH THE UNDERDOG" STAGE—NIGHT*
The Bleek Quintet, minus Shadow, takes the bandstand to applause and jumps right into it.
ANGLE—CLUB
Rod and Madlock escort Giant through the club.
CLOSE—BLEEK
He sees this.

                                                          CUT TO:

70   **EXT:** *BACK ALLEY—NIGHT*
Giant is being pummeled by blow after blow. He screams.

                                                          CUT TO:

70A **INT:** *STAGE—NIGHT*
Bleek hears something.

GIANT (OS)
BLEEK.

CUT TO:

70B **EXT:** *BACK ALLEY—NIGHT*
Eggy and Born Knowledge tell Roberto to scram as they block the backstage door. Giant still screams as the multitude of fists rain down on him like a thunderstorm.

CUT TO:

70C **INT:** *STAGE—NIGHT*

GIANT (OS)
HELP ME, BLEEK. HELP ME.

Bleek hears the screams; he understands exactly what is happening. The audience hears too, and wonders what the hell is going on. Bleek looks at the band.

BLEEK
Louder.

The band plays *louder* and *faster*.
Here we have a TIGHT MONTAGE, INTERCUTTING the band playing with Giant getting the shit kicked out of him. Bleek is trying all he can to drown out the wailing of his friend.

CUT TO:

70D **EXT:** *BACK ALLEY—NIGHT*
Madlock and Rod stand above a bloody pulp that used to be Giant. In SLOW MOTION Rod winds up his Sunday punch. He rears back and brings his fist from way back in Alabama; it gains speed coming up through North Carolina in a crash collision with Giant's head. We

SMASH CUT TO:

70E **INT:** *"BENEATH THE UNDERDOG" STAGE—NIGHT*
CLOSE—CYMBAL

GIANT (OS)
BLEEK.

Rhythm does a cymbal crash. Bleek leaves the bandstand while the band continues to play.
ANGLE—BACKSTAGE DOOR
The door is blocked by Eggy and Born Knowledge.

BLEEK
Move outta the way.

EGGY
Bleek. Go in peace. I'm asking you, go in peace.
Bleek pushes forward.

BORN KNOWLEDGE
Go on. It won't be pretty.

71 **EXT:** *BACK ALLEY—NIGHT*
Madlock and Rod hover over an unconscious Giant, who is choking on his own blood. Sugar Ray didn't beat Jake LaMotta this bad.
Bleek rushes to Giant and lifts his head off the cold and wet sidewalk.

BLEEK
I WAS GETTING HIM THE MONEY TONIGHT.

MADLOCK
Too little. Too late.

ROD

He's not dead. He'll be alright.

Bleek takes a wild swing and connects with Rod's cheek.

ROD

Now, why did you do that?

MADLOCK

We're gonna have to give you some of this too.

Bleek takes a boxing stance and before he can get off one punch, Madlock pops him five quick times square on right in the *mouth. Blood* and *teeth* fly everwhere. Bleek flies back like a projectile and lands on top of some garbage cans next to Giant.

ANGLE—BACKSTAGE DOOR

Eggy and Born Knowledge, no longer able to keep the crowd in, open the door.

72 **EXT:** *BACK ALLEY—NIGHT*

The crowd, led by Shadow, rushes into the alley. Rita faints into the arms of Butterbean, and Clarke starts screaming like her child has been murdered.

ANGLE—ALLEY

At the end of the alley, Rod and Madlock slowly walk away, never looking back.

ANGLE—CROWD

Moe and Josh fight their way through the crowd and look at Giant and Bleek.

MOE

NOT IN THE MOUTH. NOT IN THE MOUTH. YOU BUSTED HIS MOUTH. YOU BUSTED HIS MOUTH.

At this point it's beyond the point of bedlam. People are yelling for "an ambulance," "call the cops," and start to push and shove.

MOE

Shadow, maybe you should get your guys and go back inside and play.

SHADOW

No.

MOE

We got a full house in there.

JOSH

Moe, let's close it up.

SHADOW

Fuck 'em.

JOSH

Moe, leave it alone.

SHADOW

We ain't playing here ever again.

MOE

Don't say that, you're upset. I understand.

SHADOW

This ain't a plantation, we're men, not slaves, and we want to be respected as such.

The band is defiant, they won't budge.

JOSH

Moe, let's close it for tonight.

MOE

Alright, alright. We're closed. Everybody go home.

FADE OUT.

FADE IN:

72A   INT: *HOSPITAL ROOM—NIGHT*

Big Stop sits at the side of Bleek's bed. Bleek's lips are the size of cantaloupes, it's fucked-up. It's killing Big Stop as it would any parent to see his son in this condition.

BIG STOP

I remember the first fight you got in. Your mother, God bless her soul, wanted me to break it up, call the cops and go speak to the parents of the kid. I felt kids are gonna fight and you musta been six or seven years old, so we were only talking about little bare fists, just skin. This was way before kids started shooting each other with Uzi's. I looked out the window and watched you go toe to toe and slug it out. Your mother never forgave me. But I must admit I felt proud. You gave the kid a bloody nose, you didn't kill him, it's a part of growing up. You ran upstairs crying, you were more scared than the kid was . . .
Wasn't that Giant?

CLOSE—BLEEK

Tears are welling up in his eyes.

CLOSE—BIG STOP

BIG STOP

I might be wrong, but I'm sure that was Giant.

72B   INT: *BLEEK'S LOFT—DAY*

The loft is a mess, stuff is everywhere. All the windows are shut, Venetian blinds closed; no sunlight can make its way into Bleek's life.

ANGLE—BLEEK

Bleek sits on the floor.

ANGLE—TRUMPET

Bleek's trumpet stands at the other side of the room.

WE WILL INTERCUT the following TWO SHOTS:

A) SLOW DOLLY INTO CLOSE-UP of Bleek as he stares at trumpet.

B) SLOW DOLLY INTO trumpet.

CLOSE—BLEEK

In SLOW MOTION, he puts the trumpet into his mouth. Bleek's lips are not as grotesque now, but the damage is still noticeable.

73   EXT: *"DIZZY CLUB"—STREET—NIGHT*

TITLE: ONE YEAR LATER

The rain is pouring down as Bleek stands across from the "DIZZY CLUB," a new and bigger jazz club than "Beneath the Underdog." On the marquee reads "THE SHADOW HENDERSON QUARTET, featuring CLARKE BENTANCOURT." A long line of people holding umbrellas wait to enter.

73A   EXT: *"DIZZY CLUB"—NIGHT*

Bleek walks across the street to Giant, who's the doorman.

BLEEK

Midget.

Giant can't believe his eyes. Bleek does not speak the same because of the damage to his mouth.

GIANT

Where have you been? Nobody hasn't seen or heard from you. How you doin'?

BLEEK

Good.

GIANT

I got this gig and I stopped gambling, but I go to meetings once a
week.

Giant looks at the trumpet case Bleek is holding.

GIANT

You gonna sit in?

BLEEK

If Shadow lets me.

GIANT

He's doing alright.

BLEEK

He always wanted to have his own shit. Good for him, I'm happy for
the brother.

Giant looks at Bleek's mouth. It's not the same, it looks funny, a lot of scar tissue,
a lot of surgery. He wants to ask Bleek about it, but he doesn't have the heart.

73B   INT: *"DIZZY CLUB"*

The band performs.

74   INT: *"DIZZY CLUB"—NIGHT*

The band, Shadow, Bottom, Left Hand, Rhythm, and Clarke are all onstage.

CLOSE—SHADOW

He has mike in hand.

SHADOW

At this time I'd like to ask Bleek Gilliam to come up.

ANGLE—BLEEK

Bleek walks from the back of the club to the stage, greeted by a very warm
applause. (PLEASE, NO STANDING OVATIONS. IT'S TOO CLICHÉ AND
DOES NOT WORK IN FILMS.)

ANGLE—STAGE

Everybody hugs Bleek as the applause continues and Clarke gives him a kiss.
Finished with the greetings, the band begins to play.

CLOSE—BLEEK

Right away you can hear Bleek has lost it, he can't play, not up to his standards.
He lost it in the alley a year ago trying to save his best friend from being killed.
Bleek can't lie to himself anymore, he's done that for a year, but beginning tonight
he accepts what he's already feared.

CLOSE—BLEEK'S MOUTH

In SLOW MOTION Bleek takes the trumpet out of his mouth.

ANGLE—STAGE

Bleek takes a bow, touches Shadow gently on the shoulder and leaves the stage.
One by one the band stops playing.

ANGLE—CLUB

The audience is silent as Bleek walks through them, past Giant and into the street.

75   EXT: *"DIZZY CLUB"—NIGHT*

It is raining harder now and Giant limps behind Bleek.

GIANT

It's alright, Bleek. It's OK.

BLEEK

I'll never play again. Never again.

GIANT

But you ain't dead. You're still *alive*.

Bleek stops and hands Giant his trumpet. He turns away.

GIANT

Bleek, where are you going?

HIGH ANGLE—STREET

Bleek walks away, leaving Giant in the street.

76 **EXT:** *INDIGO'S APARTMENT—NIGHT*

Bleek is ringing Indigo's buzzer, his hand stays on the bell. He has an urgency about him, like he's running out of time.

INDIGO (VO)

Who is it?

BLEEK

Me. Bleek.

INDIGO (VO)

Bleek!

CLOSE—BLEEK

Bleek's face is wet from the rain and he dries it with his hands.

ANGLE—DOOR

Indigo opens the door; she's dressed in a nightgown.

INDIGO

Bleek.

BLEEK

May I come in?

She fully opens the door.

77 **INT:** *INDIGO'S APARTMENT—NIGHT*

INDIGO

You didn't return my calls, my letters, refused my visits.

BLEEK

It doesn't matter.

INDIGO

It doesn't matter?

Indigo goes after him right away. She's been waiting for the moment.

INDIGO

I haven't heard from you in over a year.

BLEEK

I didn't want to see anyone. I only saw my father.

INDIGO

You always have been a selfish person.

BLEEK

I admit it. All artists are. I was a selfish motherfucker.

INDIGO

You didn't trust me. You didn't know me, nor talk to me. I would have never, never done anything to stop you from doing what you had to do.

BLEEK

I know now.

INDIGO

Now? What about the past year? Now, you just show up.

BLEEK

Do ya want me to leave?

INDIGO

Yes! Back then it could have been so easy. You'll never be able to play again, and now you want my love. Bleek, you had my love then, you had your music. You had both.

Bleek is a desperate man, and he does what desperate men do: *Beg* and *plead*. Indigo pushes Bleek toward the door.

BLEEK

You gotta let me redeem myself.

INDIGO

Redemption. The only reason you're here is because you can't play anymore and Clarke is with Shadow.

He puts his hands on Indigo's shoulders.

INDIGO

Don't, Bleek.

BLEEK

I once read, I forget where, a married couple was on a plane and it was going down, about to crash into the sea. Without thinking, they tore off their clothes and began to make love ferociously, right there in their seats, oblivious to anyone and everything. They didn't care. The plane was about to crash and they all would be dead.

Bleek begins to pull Indigo closer to him.

INDIGO

Get off me, Bleek.

BLEEK

They loved each other dearly and wanted to be together if they had to go. That plane, by some miracle, avoided crashing, but how were they to know?

Bleek is now pressed up against Indigo as she struggles.

CLOSE—BLEEK AND INDIGO

BLEEK

I want to be with you.

Indigo has started to cry.

INDIGO

I don't know. I don't know. It's been too long.

He starts to kiss her.

BLEEK

You. Me. A son.

INDIGO

Go tell that to somebody else. You want me to save your life, that's what you're asking. What about my life? What about my life this past year?

BLEEK

You want me to roll back the clock? I can't do that. But I can do something about now.

Bleek lifts Indigo up and she locks her legs around his waist. Standing up, Bleek and Indigo *make love*, not boning, not the "mo' better," but *make love*, like their two very lives depended on it.

CUT TO:

77A   CLOSE—ELECTRON MICROSCOPIC SHOT

Using one of the HIGH-POWERED MICROSCOPE JAMMIES, WE SEE the moment of *conception*. The sperm meets the egg.

SMASH CUT TO:

77B   **INT:** *INDIGO'S APARTMENT—NIGHT*
CLOSE—INDIGO
She screams for joy.

CUT TO:

78   THE MONTAGE FINALE
The end of this film will be seven minutes and forty-six seconds long. Why? Because that's the length of "Love Supreme," the monumental jazz recording of John Coltrane. This piece, "Love Supreme," will play over, underneath and with the MONTAGE which will cover the span of eight years.

78A   **INT:** *BLEEK'S LOFT—DAY*
Indigo is pregnant (showing).

78B   **INT:** *BLEEK'S LOFT—DAY*
Bleek looks at his trumpet.

78C   **EXT:** *BLEEK'S ROOF—DAY*
Bleek and Indigo get married at a small wedding. Giant is the best man.

78D   **EXT:** *BROOKLYN BRIDGE—DAY*
Bleek and Indigo walk over the Brooklyn Bridge.

78E   **INT:** *BIG STOP'S HOUSE—DAY*
Indigo in labor.

78F   **EXT:** *HOSPITAL—DAY*
Bleek rushes Indigo to the hospital.

78G   **INT:** *HOSPITAL—DELIVERY ROOM—DAY*
Indigo is giving birth.

78H   **INT:** *HOSPITAL—DELIVERY ROOM—DAY*
Bleek watches.

78I   **INT:** *HOSPITAL—DELIVERY ROOM—DAY*
Their son pops out of Indigo.

78J   **INT:** *HOSPITAL—DELIVERY ROOM—DAY*
Bleek holds his son.

78K   **EXT:** *BIG STOP'S HOUSE—DAY*
Bleek brings his son and wife home.

78L   **INT:** *BIG STOP'S HOUSE—DAY*
Bleek at home; he's a music teacher.

78M   **INT:** *BIG STOP'S HOUSE—DAY*
Big Stop gives his grandson, MILES, a baseball glove.

78N   **INT:** *BIG STOP'S HOUSE—DAY*
Miles is crawling.

78O   **INT:** *BIG STOP'S HOUSE—DAY*
Miles is walking.

78P   **EXT:** *SCHOOL—DAY*
Bleek and Indigo walk with Miles on first day of nursery school.

78Q   **INT:** *BIG STOP'S HOUSE—DAY*
Miles' birthday party; he's three years old.

78R   **INT:** *BIG STOP'S HOUSE—DAY*
Bleek is giving his son trumpet lessons and we

CUT TO:

79 **EXT:** *BIG STOP'S HOUSE—DAY*
Four kids are yelling at the top of their lungs. These are the same four kids WE
SAW at the beginning of the movie.

> **TYRONE**
> Yo, Miles. Yo, Miles. Yo, Miles. Come on out to play. Come on out to
> play.

> **JOE**
> We're wasting time on him.

ANGLE—WINDOW

> **INDIGO**
> Boys! Boys! Please be quiet.

CLOSE—TYRONE

> **TYRONE**
> Sorry, Mrs. Gilliam. We want to know if Miles can come out?

CLOSE—INDIGO

> **INDIGO**
> I understand that, but your noise has to stop.

She pulls her head back in.

80 **INT:** *BIG STOP'S HOUSE—DAY*
WE DOLLY as Indigo leads us to MILES, eight years old, and he's practicing his
scales on his trumpet under the watchful eye of his father.

> **INDIGO**
> Miles, didn't I tell your hoodlum friends not to come around here?

> **BLEEK**
> Aw, Indigo. Leave the boy alone.

> **MILES**
> Can I go out now?

> **INDIGO**
> Not until you finish your practice.

> **MILES**
> What about then?

> **INDIGO**
> We'll see.

> **TYRONE (OS)**
> Yo, Miles. Yo, Miles.

Miles looks at his father.

> **BLEEK**
> We're done for the day.

Before Indigo can protest, Miles has grabbed his baseball glove, cap, and runs
out.

ANGLE—WINDOW
Bleek takes Indigo by the hand and goes to the window.

> **BLEEK**
> Let the boy have some fun.

80A **EXT:** *BIG STOP'S STREET—DAY*
ANGLE—BLEEK'S, INDIGO'S POV
Miles and his friends run down the block to the park, and it looks like they're
having the time of their lives.
CLOSE—BLEEK AND INDIGO

Bleek and Indigo stand arm in arm, in the window; he tries to remember what it felt like to be that young, playing baseball with Big Stop, not having a care in the world.

                                                                FADE OUT.

THE END

f i v e

mo'
B E T T E R
STORYBOARDS

 have a hunch—a director's hunch—that the most discussed scene in *Mo' Better Blues* will be the one that intercuts Bleek making love to Indigo and to Clarke.

Bleek's life is like this: he has two female friends and they both know about each other. The women can protest, but Bleek is in the driver's seat. He's a prize catch and he knows it. To him, Clarke and Indigo are interchangeable, to be called upon whenever. This is not to say I agree with his program, but it's his program.

In writing this scene, I wanted Indigo and Clarke to become one, a blur. I wanted the audience to lose track of where Indigo begins and Clarke ends. This distinction goes by Bleek also. He slips up, calling each woman by the other's name. All hell breaks loose. Both women fire him up. Bleek's defenseless; there is nothing he can do, and not much he can say, except what men usually say in these situations, just "fuck it."

We shot this scene over the course of two nights. The first night was tense. It got off to rocky start when I politely asked Denzel to take his shirt off. He told me flatly, no, that he had taken his shirt off in the other love scenes, and that was enough. I was in a no-win situation. It wasn't the time for me to play "I'm the producer, I'm the director"; Denzel wasn't taking his shirt off and that was it. I didn't want to jeopardize the shoot or our working relationship, so I said, fine, keep your shirt on and let's go.

The second night went smoother. Joie and Cynda were on the set together most of the night. For each setup they interchanged positions quickly. On some takes, they fed each other lines from off-screen. The entire sequence was shot in order, following the storyboards closely. This is not the way I usually work, but it was necessary given the importance of continuity in the scene.

We boarded two other scenes for *Mo' Better Blues:*

1. Giant bicycles down the street and crashes into a car door.
2. Giant and Bleek are beaten up in the alley behind Beneath the Underdog.

Jeff Balsmeyer, the storyboard artist we used on *Do the Right Thing*, came back for *Mo' Better Blues.* As before, in preproduction, Ernest and I discussed which scenes should be storyboarded. We gave Jeff a script, along with shot lists for two scenes that required boards. For the Bleek/Indigo/Clarke love scene, he worked directly from the script. When Jeff came back with the sketches, we knew we had a winner. All that was left to do was to follow the boards and get the performances.

The first time I saw the scene cut together, I thought it might confuse audiences. Would they think it was a ménage à trois? I asked folks in the editing room; they didn't find it confusing. Of course, asking people who work on the film, day in, day out, is not the same as asking a cold audience.

For me, this scene marks the decline of Bleek's character, though he does redeem himself, his life, by the end of the film. Bleek was always on his p's and q's, but eventually he slips up, all men do, we all do. Covering your tracks is too much work. Bleek got his names mixed up, but it could have been a bobbie pin, the faint scent of perfume, hair on a comb. Bleek got busted. And when that happens, all we can really, really do is shut up, take that *good* cussing out. And when the tirade is over, say, I'm sorry, I didn't mean it, it's you I love, or the other route, "fuck it." Bleek's the lucky one. He comes around by the end of the movie. A lot of men don't.

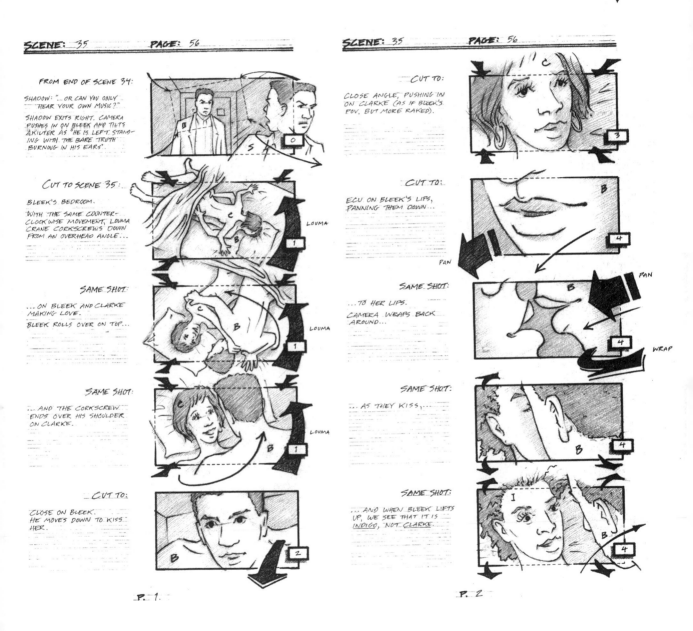

SCENE: 35   PAGE: 56

FROM END OF SCENE 34:

SHADOW: "...OR CAN YOU ONLY HEAR YOUR OWN MUSIC?"

SHADOW EXITS RIGHT. CAMERA PUSHES IN ON BLEEK AND TILTS AKILTER AS "HE IS LEFT STANDING WITH THE BARE TRUTH BURNING IN HIS EARS".

CUT TO SCENE 35:

BLEEK'S BEDROOM.

WITH THE SAME COUNTER-CLOCKWISE MOVEMENT, LOUMA CRANE CORKSCREWS DOWN FROM AN OVERHEAD ANGLE...

SAME SHOT:

...ON BLEEK AND CLARKE MAKING LOVE.
BLEEK ROLLS OVER ON TOP...

SAME SHOT:

...AND THE CORKSCREW ENDS OVER HIS SHOULDER ON CLARKE.

CUT TO:

CLOSE ON BLEEK.
HE MOVES DOWN TO KISS HER.

P. 1.

SCENE: 35   PAGE: 56

CUT TO:

CLOSE ANGLE, PUSHING IN ON CLARKE (AS IF BLEEK'S POV, BUT MORE RAKED).

CUT TO:

ECU ON BLEEK'S LIPS, PANNING THEM DOWN...

SAME SHOT:

...TO HER LIPS.
CAMERA WRAPS BACK AROUND...

SAME SHOT:

...AS THEY KISS,...

SAME SHOT:

...AND WHEN BLEEK LIFTS UP, WE SEE THAT IT IS INDIGO, NOT CLARKE.

P. 2

MO'
BETTER
BLUES

SCENE: 35   PAGE: 56

CUT TO:

REVERSE. BLEEK BLINKS.
THE TWO ROLL OVER....

(panel 5)

SAME SHOT:

...AND IT'S CLARKE
AGAIN.

NOTE: THE FOLLOWING SHOTS
THRU #15 WILL BE A QUICK-
CUTTING MONTAGE IN WHICH
CLARKE AND INDIGO INTER-
CHANGE, BECOME ONE AND
THE SAME.

(panel 5)

CUT TO:

A FLURRY OF SHEETS.

(panel 6)

CUT TO:

INTERTWINED LIMBS,
ROLLING AGAIN.

(panel 7)

CUT TO:

A HEAD HITS A PILLOW,
AND IT'S INDIGO.

(panel 8)

P. 3

SCENE: 35   PAGE: 56

CUT TO:

BLEEK'S EYES MOVE INTO
AN ECU — LOOKING?
         FANTASIZING?
CONFUSED?

(panel 9)

CUT TO:

BLEEK'S HAND PULLS
INDIGO'S NECK UP OUT
OF FRAME.

(panel 10)

CUT TO:

WITH THE SAME MOVEMENT,
CLARKE COMES UP AND
SMELLS BLEEK'S NECK.

SHE THEN CROSSES BE-
HIND HIM.

(panel 11)

CUT TO:

REVERSE, ON BLEEK, AS
CLARKE PASSES RIGHT.

(panel 12)

CUT TO:

ANGLE OVER BLEEK — AND
IT'S INDIGO WHO COMES OUT
THE OTHER SIDE, SMELLING
HIS HAIR.

(panel 13)

P. 4

MO'
BETTER
BLUES

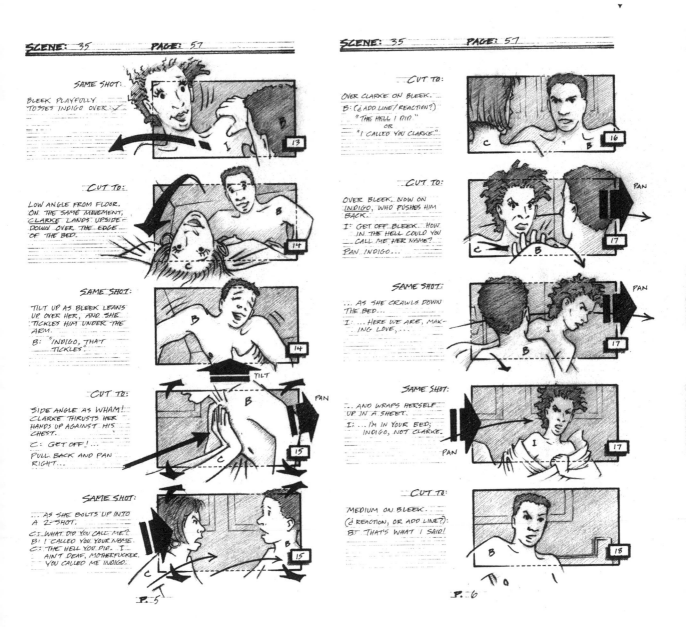

SCENE: 35   PAGE: 57

SAME SHOT:
BLEEK PLAYFULLY TOSSES INDIGO OVER. — 13

CUT TO:
LOW ANGLE FROM FLOOR. ON THE SAME MOVEMENT, CLARKE LANDS UPSIDE-DOWN OVER THE EDGE OF THE BED. 14

SAME SHOT:
TILT UP AS BLEEK LEANS UP OVER HER, AND SHE TICKLES HIM UNDER THE ARM.
B: "INDIGO, THAT TICKLES." 14

CUT TO:
SIDE ANGLE AS WHAM! CLARKE THRUSTS HER HANDS UP AGAINST HIS CHEST.
C: GET OFF! ...
PULL BACK AND PAN RIGHT... 15

SAME SHOT:
...AS SHE BOLTS UP INTO A 2-SHOT.
C: WHAT DID YOU CALL ME?
B: I CALLED YOU YOUR NAME.
C: THE HELL YOU DID. I AIN'T DEAF, MOTHERFUCKER. YOU CALLED ME INDIGO. 15
P. 5

SCENE: 35   PAGE: 57

CUT TO:
OVER CLARKE ON BLEEK.
B: (¿ADD LINE/ REACTION?)
"THE HELL I DID."
OR
"I CALLED YOU CLARKE." 16

CUT TO:
OVER BLEEK, NOW ON INDIGO, WHO PUSHES HIM BACK.
I: GET OFF, BLEEK. HOW IN THE HELL COULD YOU CALL ME HER NAME?
PAN INDIGO... PAN 17

SAME SHOT:
...AS SHE CRAWLS DOWN THE BED...
I: ...HERE WE ARE, MAKING LOVE,... PAN 17

SAME SHOT:
...AND WRAPS HERSELF UP IN A SHEET.
I: ...I'M IN YOUR BED; INDIGO, NOT CLARKE.
PAN 17

CUT TO:
MEDIUM ON BLEEK.
(¿REACTION, OR ADD LINE?):
B: THAT'S WHAT I SAID! 18
P. 6

SCENE: 35   PAGE: 57-58

CUT TO:

MATCHED ANGLE ON CLARKE.
C: I'M CLARKE, NOT INDIGO.
   YOU CAN PRACTICE FOR 8
   HOURS STRAIGHT, BUT YOU
   CAN'T SPEND THE LITTLE
   EXTRA TIME IT TAKES TO
   BUY ME AND YOUR OTHER
   WOMAN A DIFFERENT DRESS.

BACK TO:

BLEEK ROLLS HIS EYES.

BACK TO:

MATCHED ANGLE ON INDIGO.
I: I DON'T LIKE IT. I DON'T
   APPRECIATE IT AND I
   DON'T LIKE TO BE DIS-
   RESPECTED.
   I'VE HAD IT.
   AND YOU SAY YOU LOVE ME.

BACK TO:

BLEEK LEANS UP.
B: I NEVER SAID THAT.

BACK TO:

INDIGO.
I: YOU DID TOO...

P. 7

SCENE: 35   PAGE: 58

BACK TO:

BLEEK.
B: WELL, I DON'T REMEMBER.

BACK TO:

MATCHED ANGLE ON CLARKE.
C: DO YOU REMEMBER SAY-
   ING YOU CARE?

CUT TO:

WIDE 2-SHOT.
B: NOW THAT I REMEMBER.
C: YOU SAY YOU CARE FOR
   ME, WHY IN THE FUCK...

SAME SHOT:

C: ...ARE YOU STILL FUCKING
   INDIGO? DON'T GIVE ME
   THAT "IT'S A DICK THING"
   SHIT EITHER.

CUT TO:

OVER CLARKE ON BLEEK.
WHAT CAN HE SAY?

P. 8

MO'
BETTER
BLUES

SCENE: 35   PAGE: 58-59

CUT TO:

OVER BLEEK ON INDIGO.

I: AND DON'T GIVE ME
   THAT "IT'S A DICK THING"
   SH!T EITHER.

CUT TO:

OVER INDIGO ON BLEEK,
WHO LOOKS AWAY.

CUT TO:

OVER BLEEK ON CLARKE.

C: WHY CAN'T YOU LOOK
   INTO MY EYES?
   WHY CAN'T YOU?

BACK TO:

OVER CLARKE ON BLEEK.

C: ... THAT'S WHERE THE
   REAL ME IS. IS IT
   TOO REAL FOR YOU?

BACK TO:

OVER BLEEK ON INDIGO.

I: YOU ALWAYS AVOID DIRECT
   EYE CONTACT. OR IS
   IT SOMETHING IN YOU
   I MIGHT SEE?...

P. 9

SCENE: 35   PAGE: 59

CUT TO:

CLOSE ON BLEEK, GLARING.
I (OS): ... THE REAL YOU?

CUT TO:

CLOSE ON CLARKE.
C: THINK ABOUT THAT.

BACK TO:

BLEEK STRUGGLES FOR
SOMETHING TO SAY, SOME-
THING TO EXPLAIN HIMSELF.
HE HAS TO DO SOMETHING.

HE GLANCES BACK AND
FORTH, THEN FIXES ON
SOMETHING OFF-LEFT.

PAN

CUT TO:

ANGLE ON TRUMPET ON
NIGHTSTAND.

AS BLEEK GRABS IT AND
STANDS UP, CAMERA PANS
UP AND SWINGS AROUND...

DOLLY BACK

SAME SHOT:

... WITH HIM AS HE TURNS
TO FACE CLARKE.

B: THE LARGEST PART OF
   MY HEART HAS ALREADY
   BEEN TAKEN, AND IF
   YOU CAN HANG WITH THAT,
   FINE. IF NOT, LET'S NOT
   PRETEND.

PAN

DOLLY BACK

P. 10

MO'
BETTER
BLUES

CUT TO:

OVER BLEEK ON CLARKE.

C: LET'S NOT PRETEND
ANYMORE.

SAME SHOT:

CLARKE TURNS AND GETS OUT
OF BED.

B (OS): FINE.

CUT TO:

REVERSE: ON SAME MOVE-
MENT, _INDIGO_ STANDS UP
INTO FRAME.

I: I CAN'T HANG.

SAME SHOT:

SHE EXITS FRAME.

B: I FUCKED UP.

O.S. WE HEAR INDIGO BRING
UP THE SUBJECT OF THE
DRESS AGAIN.

SAME SHOT:

BLEEK TURNS AND BEGINS
TO PLAY.

CUT TO:

REVERSE, OVER BLEEK PLAY-
ING, WITH CLARKE WALKING
OUT THE DOOR, CARRYING
ON ABOUT THE DRESS.

BLEEK SWINGS HIS HORN.
INTO CAMERA...

SAME SHOT:

... FILLING THE FRAME.

**MO'
BETTER
BLUES**

FEATURE FILMS

SHE'S GOTTA HAVE IT ● 1986
SCHOOL DAZE ● 1988
DO THE RIGHT THING ● 1989
MO' BETTER BLUES ● 1990
JUNGLE FEVER ● Pre-production

MUSIC VIDEOS

SHE'S GOTTA HAVE IT ● *NOLA*—1986
MILES DAVIS ● *TUTU MEDLEY*—1986
BRANFORD MARSALIS ● *ROYAL GARDEN BLUES*—1986
ANITA BAKER ● *NO ONE IN THE WORLD*—1987
E.U. ● *DA BUTT*—1988
THE RAYS ● *BE ALONE TONIGHT*—1988
PHYLLIS HYMAN ● *BE ONE*—1988
KEITH JOHN ● *I CAN ONLY BE ME*—1988
STEEL PULSE ● *REACHIN' OUT*—1988
E.U. ● *BUCK WILD*—1989
PUBLIC ENEMY ● *FIGHT THE POWER*—1989
PERRI ● *FEEL SO GOOD*—1989
TRACY CHAPMAN ● *BORN TO FIGHT*—1989

SHORT FILMS

MTV ● Five one-minute spots—1986
HORN OF PLENTY ● "Saturday Night Live"—1986

STUDENT FILMS
(New York University)

THE ANSWER ● 1980
SARAH ● 1981
JOE'S BED-STUY BARBERSHOP: WE CUT HEADS ● 1982

COMMERCIALS
1988
HANG TIME ● AIR JORDAN / NIKE
COVER ● AIR JORDAN / NIKE
CHARLES BARKLEY ● NIKE

**MO'
BETTER
BLUES**

1989
RAPPIN ● AIR JORDAN / NIKE
CAN/CAN'T ● AIR JORDAN / NIKE
NOLA ● AIR JORDAN / NIKE
1990
OPINIONS ● AIR JORDAN / NIKE
AERODYNAMICS ● AIR JORDAN / NIKE
MARS BEDROOM ● AIR JORDAN/NIKE
JESSE JACKSON *DRUGS* ● New York State Primary

BOOKS

SPIKE LEE'S GOTTA HAVE IT: Inside Guerilla Filmmaking
1987
UPLIFT THE RACE: The Construction of School Daze
1988
DO THE RIGHT THING: A Spike Lee Joint
1989
MO' BETTER BLUES
1990

mo'

BETTER BLUES
CREDITS

CAST

Bleek	Denzel Washington
Giant	Spike Lee
Shadow Henderson	Wesley Snipes
Left Hand Lacey	Giancarlo Esposito
Butterbean Jones	Robin Harris
Indigo	Joie Lee
Bottom Hammer	Bill Nunn
Moe Flatbush	John Turturro
Big Stop Gilliam	Dick Anthony Williams
Clarke	Cynda Williams
Josh Flatbush	Nicholas Turturro
Rhythm	Jeff 'Tain' Watts
Madlock	Samuel L. Jackson
Rod	Leonard Thomas
Eggy	Charles Q. Murphy
Born Knowledge	Steve White
Petey	Rubén Blades
Lillian Gilliam	Abbey Lincoln
Jeanne	Linda Hawkins
Rita	Raye Dowell
Cora	Angela Hall
Roberto	Coati Mundi
Young Bleek/Miles	Zakee L. Howze

Tyrone	Deon Richmond
Sam	Terrence Williams
Joe	Raymond Thomas
Benny	Sheldon Turnipseed
Louis	Christopher Skeffrey
Shanika	Anaysha Figueroa
Miles at birth	Darryl M. Wonge, Jr.
Miles at one year old	Jelani Asar Snipes
Miles at three years old	Glenn Williams, III
Miles at five years old	Arnold Cromer
Smith	Leon Addison Brown
Cooley	Scot Anthony Robinson
Minister	Rev. Herbert Daughtry
Father of the Bride	Bill Lee
Party Guest	Branford Marsalis
Jimmy the Busboy	Douglas Bourne
Club Patrons	Tracy Camilla Johns
	John Canada Terrell
	Monty Ross
	Carol M. Wiggins
	Isabella
	Mamie Louis Anderson
Big Stop's Friend	Joe Seneca
Taxi Driver	John Sobestanovich

Produced, Written And Directed By   Spike Lee
Co-Producer   Monty Ross
Line Producer   Jon Kilik
Photographed By   Ernest Dickerson
Original Music Score   Bill Lee
Editor   Sam Pollard
Production Design   Wynn Thomas
Casting   Robi Reed
Costume Design   Ruth Carter
Sound Design   Skip Lievsay

Production Supervisor   Preston Holmes
Unit/Location Manager   Brent Owens
1st Assistant Director   Randy Fletcher
2nd Assistant Director   H. H. Cooper
                                     Dale Pierce-Johnson

Production Office Coordinator   Debra D. Jeffreys
Assistant Production Office   Alysse Bezahler
   Coordinator
40 Acres Production Coordinator   Susan D. Fowler
Production Secretary   Desirée Jellerette
Unit Publicist   Anna Southall

Production Comptroller   Robert Nickson
Auditor   Eric Oden
Assistant Auditor   Patricia Holmes
                                     Leticia Lee

Script/Continuity   Nike Zachmanoglou

Camera Operator   John Newby
1st Assistant Camera   Pam Katz
                                     Jonathan Burkhart
2nd Assistant Camera   Henry Adebonojo
                                     Andrew Harris
Steadicam Operators   Ted Churchill
                                     Bob Gorelick
                                     Larry McConkey
Additional Camera Operators   Phil Oeticker
                                     George Pattison
Additional 1st Assistant Camera   Susan Starr
                                     Joan Zierler
Additional 2nd Assistant Camera   Myra-Lee Cohen
                                     Paul Reuter
Still Photography   David Lee

MO'
BETTER
BLUES

Camera Trainees	Leslie Saltus
	Floyd A. B. Rance III
Sound Recordist	Frank Stettner
Boom Operator	Andrew Schmetterling
Cable Man/Playback	Abdul Abbott
Assistant Art Directors	Charles McClennahan
	Michael T. Roberts
Art Department Coordinator	Pam Stephens
Storyboard Artist	Jeff Balsmeyer
Set Decorator	Ted Glass
Leadman	Bruce Lee Gross
2nd Dresser	Joan Brocksmidt
Set Dressers	Bill Butler
	Michael Leather
	Nancy Boytos
	Mark Selemon
Assistant to the Set Decorator	Kimberley Ann Buckley
Property Master	Octavio Molina
1st Assistant Props	Kevin Ladson
2nd Assistant Props	Philip Michelson
Gaffer	Charles Houston
Best Boy	Valerie DeSalvo
Electrics	John Mitchell
	John O'Malley
	Keith Salkowski
Electric Trainee	Beverly Cable
Pre-Rigging Gaffer	Martin Andrews
Dimmer Board Operator	Christian Epps
Additional Electric	Derek McKane
Additional Grips	David Noble
	Dan Finn
Key Grip	Bob Andres
Dolly Grip	Tom Kudlek
Best Boy	Carl Peterson
Grips	Ed Newins, Jr.
	Marcus Turner
Louma Crane Technician	Stuart Allen
Grip Trainee	Lois Thompson
Construction Coordinator	Martin Bernstein
Key Set Builder	Ken Nelson
Set Builders	Rodney Clark
	Mike Curry, Jr.
	John Grimolizzi
	Harold Horn

	Tim Main
	Sal Sirico
Key Construction Grip	Carl Prinzi
Construction Grips	Paul Wardwell
	Robert Woods, Jr.
Scenic Chargeman	Jeffrey L. Glave
Scenic Shopwoman	Rosalle Russino
Scenic Shopman	James Geyer
Camera Scenic	Jane Asch
Scenic Artists	Mary Citarella
	Eva Davy
	Ellen Doak
	Judith A. Evans
	Gary Jennings
	Joyce Kubalak
	Virginia Lim
	Sherryl Sachs
	Charlene Shildmeyer
Scenic Sculptor	Sara D'Allesandro
Apprentice Scenic	Wilbur L. Ball
Extras Casting	Andrea Reed
	Tracy Vilar
Casting Assistant	Paulette Clark
Assistant Location Managers	Dale T. Watkins
	Bil Haley-Freeman
Locations Assistant	Eric Barry Klein
Assistants to the Costume Designer	Beulah Jones-Black
	Donna Berwick
Wardrobe Supervisor	Susie Money
Wardrobe Assistant	Lisa Frucht
Wardrobe Assistants	Miriam Wong
	Jennifer Lax
Make-Up	Matiki Anoff
Men's Hairdresser	Larry Cherry
Women's Hairdresser	Clifford Booker
Special F/X Make-Up	Tom Brumberger
Additional Make-Up	Margie Durand
	Debbie Deas
Technical Consultants	Terence Blanchard
	Michael Fleming
	Donald Harrison
	Bill Lee
1st Assistant Editor	Brunilda Torres

| Assistant Editor | Leander T. Sales |
| Apprentice Editor | Donna Myers-Rambharose |

| Dailies Projectionist | Michael Gaynor |
| Dailies Projectionist's Assistant | Harold Williams |

Sound Editors	Philip Stockton
	Kevin Lee, M.P.S.E.
ADR Editors	Gail Showalter
	Pam Demetrius

Foley Editors	Bruce Pross
	Frank Kern
Foley Artist	Marko Constanzo

| Music Editor | Alex Steyermark |
| Assistant Music Editor | James Flatto |

Assistant Sound Editors	Brian Johnson
	Gregory L. Speed
	Bill Docker
Apprentice Sound Editors	Jann McClary

Stunt Coordinator	Jeff Ward
Utility Stunt	Roy Farfel
	David Lomax
	Elliot Santiago
Special Effects Coordinator	Tom Newton
Special Effects	Michael Benson
	Will Scheck
	Chris Skutch

Transportation Captain	James Leavey
Drivers	Harry Leavey
	Willi Gaskins
	Charlie Hoffman
	Tom Newins
	Martin Whitfield

Production Assistants—40 Acres	Yolanda Busbee
	Audra Smith
Assistant to Mr. Lee	Earl Smith
Assistant to Mr. Washington	Larry Mims

| Production Assistants—Office | Traci Proctor |
| | Shari L. Carpenter |

Production Assistants—Set	Eric Daniel
	Michael Ellis
	Erik Knight

Fred Nielsen
Kia Puriefoy
Doug Watson

Craft Service

Lee Davis
Van A. Hayden
Daryl Patterson

Production Assistant—Art
  Department

Marcia Brown

Production Assistant—
  Construction

Peter Swain

Production Assistant—Shop
Production Assistant—Wardrobe

Carmen Griffin
Rita McGhee
Janinea Shelton

Production Assistant—Sound
Production Assistant—Parking

Rosa Howell-Thornhill
Brian Harris

Interns

Wanda Brooks
Jeffrey Byrd
Melvin Tyrone Clarke
Lyle Dickey
Kristen M. Johnson
Damon Jones
Palesa Ka Letlaka
Janice Kambara
Karen Mason
Tiffany McClinn
Ayesha Morales
Simona Ross
Amada R. Sandoval
Winsome GM Sinclair
Kevin A. Smith
Susan Stuart
Latanya White